Praise for the Sandler Selling System

"I went to a meeting with a former client with whom we were doing zero business, and I walked out the door with $13,000 worth of orders. Deciding to implement Sandler as a communication style in our company is probably the single best decision I've ever made."

—Jeff Tempone, *CEO, East Coast Refrigeration*

"We were at a turning point, getting ready to sell the company. What we learned from Sandler transformed our entire organization. We went from 'winging it' to creating a series of measurable processes that worked. After we signed on with Sandler, we started figuring out how much it cost us to do business with each customer, and that helped us to make better business decisions. The Sandler approach really is a metrics-driven approach. We finally realized that the Sandler way of doing business applies to the entire organization. It became part of our working culture."

—CaSh Wong, *CEO, Shing Digital*

"I actually see Sandler Training as my competitive advantage. Where all my competitors are out there running around all over town, writing proposals, doing free consulting, I'm sitting in my office and I'm making cold calls, I'm talking to people, getting it done in a lot less time than the rest of them. I know I'm spending a lot less effort on it. I'm getting the budgets that clients are willing to spend, and I'm able to deliver on the results I promise them as well."

—Jarrod Goddard, *President, Net Shift Media*

"Once you embrace the philosophy of Sandler, you can't turn it off when you go home. It helps in your personal life and we believe in it."

—Greg Mack, *Business Unit Manager, Toshiba*

"We have better relationships, more long-term relationships with our customers. The whole system does really work, and we're seeing some great success."

—Mark Tucker, *Vice President, Sales and Sales Planning, BlueRhino*

YOU CAN'T TEACH A KID TO RIDE A BIKE AT A SEMINAR

Sandler Training's 7-Step System
for Successful Selling

SECOND EDITION

David H. Sandler

Founder, Sandler Training

Updated and with a Foreword by
David H. Mattson, CEO, Sandler Training

New York Chicago San Francisco Athens London Madrid
Mexico City Milan New Delhi Singapore Sydney Toronto

The first printing of the first edition was published by Dutton, an imprint of Dutton Signet, a division of Penguin Books. All subsequent printings of the first edition were published by Bay Head Publishing Inc.

12   LCR   21 20

ISBN   978-0-07-184782-7
MHID   0-07-184782-0

e-ISBN   978-0-07-184783-4
e-MHID   0-07-184783-9

Library of Congress Cataloging-in-Publication Data

Sandler, David H.
    You can't teach a kid to ride a bike at a seminar : Sandler training's 7-step system for successful selling / David Sandler and David Mattson. — 2nd edition.
        pages cm
        ISBN 978-0-07-184782-7 (alk. paper) — ISBN 0-07-184782-0
        1. Selling. I. Mattson, David. II. Title.
        HF5438.25.S264 2015
        658.85—dc23
                                                                    2015001216

McGraw-Hill Education books are available at special quantity discounts to use as premiums and sales promotions or for use in corporate training programs. To contact a representative, please visit the Contact Us pages at www.mhprofessional.com.

CONTENTS

BY DAVID H. MATTSON, CEO, SANDLER TRAINING

More than four decades ago, David Sandler made his first foray into the personal development and sales training business. And promptly failed.

Among the most important of what the world would later come to call the Sandler Selling Rules is this one: *You have to learn to fail, to win.* It is easy to forget now that that rule, like all of the rules that support the Sandler Selling System, was the product of David Sandler's direct personal experience. Learning to fail meant "going for the no"—a concept you'll be encountering in this book—but even before that, it meant being honest with himself about whether what he was doing was actually working. And at first, what he was doing really *wasn't* working. He replicated what he observed other professional salespeople doing, but he didn't get the results that he was seeking. Before long, he found himself beaten down, with his self-esteem at an all-time low.

Sandler did some soul-searching, and he concluded that the techniques he had been taught were tired ones—so tired that prospects could see where he was going and would throw up objections and roadblocks that made his sales process even more difficult than it already was. David's biggest issue, he realized, was that he didn't have a playbook that he could follow in a consistent manner.

The playbook he ended up creating for himself, and sharing with others, transformed the sales training industry.

It has helped literally millions of salespeople to take their careers to new levels of prosperity. And the book you are holding in your hands has become an enduring business classic, in large part because it gives such a compelling summary of that playbook.

Sandler Training is today the leader in the industry that David Sandler reinvented. In bringing this book, his final project, into the twenty-first century, I have not tried to alter his voice or the fundamentals of his message. Where it seemed appropriate to offer an insight or a best practice that reflects the way the Sandler Selling System is executed today, I have done so in sidebars separate from his story, using a different typeface, so that my voice and his can be distinguished easily. These sidebars are identified as "Sandler Selling Tips."

David Sandler was one of the true pioneers in selling. He was the first in our industry to move from a "seminar training" model to a "reinforcement training" model. He made this change for those who wanted to take their own personal development to the next level. He invented the Sandler President's Club, basically a group of people who are willing to participate in ongoing reinforcement training over time, as opposed to a one-time content dump. Sandler did this because he found that people had attended his seminars, and gotten excited, but they simply couldn't implement everything that was taught. There was so much to learn that David began taking more of a collegiate approach, giving them more content over time. That's still how we deliver his material.

David also brought the concept of "pain" to the forefront of the selling industry. Since that time, other companies have tried to replicate the idea of pain and incorporate it into what they do, but David was the first to introduce it as part of a selling model and the first to bring the "doctor" analogy to the sales process.

Most important, though, was the psychology woven into the Sandler sales process.

Even today, most sales training companies still focus on what you as a salesperson should *say*. David was the first to focus on how you should *think*. Many sales training organizations provide scripts that sound great in class but are unrealistic in real-time interactions with prospects or customers. David taught you how to think in different circumstances, knowing full well that the words you chose would change with each situation or with each buyer profile. And he also changed how you thought about yourself. With the Success triangle (the behaviors, attitudes, and techniques needed to succeed), Sandler had a winning combination. It all boils down to a flexible, conversational sales model that doesn't require you to memorize a tight script—which is useless anyway. These days, I call the Sandler Selling System a "sales GPS." It gets you where you need to go.

David believed that salespeople are made, not born. He believed that we don't have to have an extrovert personality to succeed in professional sales, and he proved that with his own example. He believed we can continually shape how we proceed and how we interact with customers throughout our careers, that we don't have to get stuck in a comfort zone. Last but not least, he believed that sales is a science, not an art form—that there are clear causes and effects.

I had the distinct privilege and honor of knowing David Sandler from 1986 until his passing in 1995. He was a great mentor and a great coach because his process was always "you focused."

Let me explain what I mean by that. Traditional sales processes have always been focused on the products, the services, the features, and the benefits. A salesperson could spend countless hours searching for unique selling points and areas of differentiation from the competition—"advantages" that might be so subtle that only a sophisticated product specialist would notice them. From the prospects' and customers' points of view, most of the vendors were very close to each other, or even identical.

David challenged us to focus not on the product or service being sold, but on the other person in the conversation, on the prospect. On the "you." He wanted us to figure out what people's issues were. He wanted to know what the gaps were between where prospects are and where they want to be. He wanted to know how the prospect wanted to buy. At the same time, he taught us how to maintain the prospect's self-esteem. He showed us how to make people feel protected and safe in sharing information that they might not have thought of before, or that they hadn't planned on sharing openly with somebody whom they had just met. He maintained the self-esteem of his own employees in just the same way.

There were three traits of David's that made it easy to work for him and operate within his culture.

First and foremost, David was selfless, a word that is probably used too much these days, but it is the only one that accurately describes him. As a coach and mentor (and of course as a salesperson), he never focused on himself. He was all about focusing on others, and he did that while being quite soft-spoken.

Another trait was that he operated with clarity. Clarity was a big part of his management style in communications and setting expectations. You knew what was important to him. He cherished loyalty, he valued hard work, and he made sure you knew where you stood at all times. You didn't have to worry about having a day or a week go by with uneasiness between you and the boss. David was very clear in sharing where we all were in terms of his vision for the future. He would provide the roadmap, or he would ask you to provide the roadmap, he would approve it, and then he'd ask you to come back and get constant feedback so you could adjust it along the way. He gave you clear guidelines from which you could operate. If you didn't get it right the first time, he was there to help you readjust. He would tell you what you did well, make you feel great about that, then start talking about the things that "we still need to do." You always felt good about what you had accomplished, and you understood the gaps you had to close in order to get to the next spot. David's clarity provided boundaries for most of his interactions with managers. It helped me move to where I knew I had to go, so I could excel in a rapid fashion.

In addition to providing clarity, David made sure you always felt safe. That was his third remarkable trait. I can't overstate the value of an employee feeling safe within an organization. Safety allows people to thrive on the things they do well, and it lets them focus on doing the things that need to get done. When you're afraid, you don't do the things that are necessary to excel to greatness. You hold back, you're hesitant, you second-guess yourself. The safety that David provided was through what he called the two Ps: protection and permission. He would protect you. He would make sure that you knew you were safe, as long as you were operating within the boundaries that you had agreed to. He knew that you might not get it right all the time. If your heart was in the right place and you did the right things, then he always regarded the outcome as a learning experience, even if it wasn't what he wanted, needed, or expected. That kind of protection allowed you the freedom to think on your own and take chances.

David's second P, permission, was also an important part of how he made you feel safe. You knew what the boundaries of your decision process were, so you knew you had permission to make decisions within those guidelines. You never felt inhibited. You never thought, "I'd better go ask him before I decide." Of course, David required you to do your due diligence, to be prudent, to be conservative, to take calculated risks. He required you to *defend* your decisions—but he always gave you permission to make them, and that meant he gave you permission to fail as well. Most people don't get their decisions 100 percent right 100 percent of the time, and David knew that. So if you stayed within the agreed-upon boundaries, you never felt as if your job was on the line.

Fortunately, the failures that came along weren't great, and when they did come, they were important learning experiences. If you had a strong opinion, and you stuck to it, and it didn't pan out, David would always respect the fact that you had tried. He knew that there were always bits and pieces of even "failed" projects and opinions that could be used for the greater good. He would extract what was useful and use it in other areas.

My own time with David Sandler was special. In the formative years of my career, he taught me how to think, how to analyze, and how to communicate. And those three gifts, I find, are what most people get out of the Sandler process.

Now, leading the company he founded, I hear two things over and over again when people tell me about their experiences with Sandler:

- "I wish I had had it 25 years ago."
- "I use Sandler in my personal life as much as I do in my professional life."

When I hear these comments—and I hear them a lot—I always think of how happy my coach and mentor would be to know that we are still getting that kind of feedback. That's David Sandler's legacy, and no one else's. I'm proud to be a part of it though.

I hope you enjoy this book as much as the hundreds of thousands before you have. I hope you keep an open mind about what David has to share with you. I hope you implement whatever makes sense to you. And I hope you use David's coaching as I did: to advance your relationship with your customer and to support your own growth as a person.

—DHM

ACKNOWLEDGMENTS

Grateful thanks for help, inspiration, support, or creative combinations of all three in preparing this second edition go out to Howard Goldstein, Yusuf Toropov, Desiree Pilachowski, Brian Sullivan, Glenn Mattson, John Rosso, Brad Freyer, Rich Chiarello, Bill Bartlett, Rochelle Carrington, Hamish Knox, Jody Williamson, Troy Elmore, Ed Staub, Dave Arch, Chuck Polin, Evan Polin, Chip Doyle, Bill Morrison, Rachel Miller, Bob Diforio, Jennifer Willard, and, last but certainly not least, Margaret Jacks.

1

FIVE STEPS TO HELP YOU MASTER THE SELLING DANCE

If you don't have a selling system of your own when you are with a prospect, you will unknowingly default to the prospect's system. The prospect's system never says: "Sold." It says: "Salesperson loses."

—DAVID H. SANDLER

No matter what business you're in, or which profession you practice, if you need to sell something to make a living, or if you rely on others to sell for you, I've got something important to tell you: You can't teach a kid to ride a bike at a seminar!

If you're interested in learning a proven system of professional selling, one that will help you feel good about saying that you sell for a living, and one that will teach you how not to sacrifice your self-esteem and dignity in front of a prospect, I guarantee you that you'll benefit from reading *You Can't Teach a Kid to Ride a Bike at a Seminar*. I am convinced that the material in this book will help you. But if you read it and decide that I'm wrong, simply call to tell us, and we'll buy the book back.

Let's go back some years to when you learned how to ride a bike. You didn't jump on a two-wheeler and take off, did you? If you were like most kids, you first had to learn *how* to ride the bike. You needed to acquire techniques and then practice mastering them. You had to balance yourself on the bike, and then you had to learn how to manipulate the bike so it responded to your needs. You had to visualize yourself riding that bike. Eventually, if you were to succeed at learning how to ride a bike, you and the bike had to become *one*.

The first time you sat on your bike, training wheels probably helped keep you from tipping over. You practiced riding day after day, balancing the bike while negotiating turns and bumps in the road. Even with training wheels, you fell off once in a while, right? But you continued to try to master the bike.

One day, even before you were an accomplished rider, you or your parents removed the training wheels, and you advanced to the next level of bike riding. At first, you felt jittery riding without the support of training wheels, but your friends were now riding solo, so it was time for you to try it too. And you did, although it took some self-talk to coax you to do it. Did it matter to you that some kids needed more time than others to learn to ride a bike? No! You had to ride that bike *now*.

Fortunately, you had someone, perhaps your parents, who steadied the bike for you while you practiced. You needed their guiding hand and their words of encouragement to keep the bike moving. You were thankful to have someone to grab the back of the seat of your bike and balance you as you pedaled the bike across the driveway or down the sidewalk. As you built up speed, the steadying hand let go. And what happened?

You fell off! Ouch, that hurt. Sometimes it hurt so much that you cried. Some days you thought it was impossible to learn to ride a bike. But you kept trying, if for no other reason than to keep up with your friends. Then one day, you sat on the seat, grabbed the handlebars of that bike, and pedaled all by yourself!

> Learning how to sell professionally is a lot like learning how to ride a bicycle. People don't learn to sell at a seminar, but the *reinforcement training* of a seminar is helpful.

Almost like magic, you had conquered the art of riding a bicycle. You and the bike had become *one*. Your body had learned the right moves. Your head, hands, and eyes all worked together, and to someone who didn't know any better, it looked as though you had been riding a bike all your life.

Occasionally, you still fell off, or you ran into a tree or a parked car, but there was never any doubt now about your ability to ride. You knew you could do it. You knew you could be good at it. All you had to do was *practice, practice, practice*. Master the techniques, improve your skills, and you'd never forget how to ride a bike. All you needed now was a little time.

Learning how to sell professionally is a lot like learning how to ride a bicycle. People don't learn to sell at a seminar, but the *reinforcement training* of a seminar is helpful. Nor do people learn how to sell from

CDs, books, and videos, but these, too, are useful tools, like training wheels or a balancing hand.

To conquer the art of professional selling, you need to learn a system. You need to master techniques (but not traditional sales techniques), and you need to be nurtured and supported—not for a day or two, but for months, if not years. Selling professionally requires the modification of your behavior and the alteration of preconceived ideas that have been ingrained in the minds of both salespeople and prospects for centuries. *Selling professionally is a process.* You can't conquer the process overnight. You can't conquer it without reinforcement training. And no two people will learn the system in the same period of time.

Unfortunately, many people believe there's a shortcut to learning how to sell professionally. By the tens of thousands, these are the people who every year attend seminars and buy audios that are produced by self-appointed sales training experts who entertain but don't teach. Some of these experts are playing off the notoriety they gained in a profession other than sales. If they teach anything at all, it's traditional sales technology jazzed up for modern times. And it doesn't work anymore! These entertainers have gleaned information from antiquated books about selling, and they extol their shtick in person, in books, on TV, online, and just about everywhere else to uncritical but often desperate people who accept it as factual, time-tested, sure-to-win sales technology.

What happens as a result? *Nothing.* Sooner or later, most of these people fall off the bike. Most never get up and try again. For a day or two following a seminar, there's a feeling of euphoria, and there's a guffaw during lunch about one of the entertainer 's stories, but long-term benefits do not occur. Consider, for example, the message of a popular sales entertainer who explains his favorite technique for making cold calls, the most baneful of sales practices: "Simply say to yourself over and over again: 'I love it! I love it! I love it!' right before you go through a strange door. It will work every time!"

Really? It never worked for me. And I tried it. If you try it, it won't work for you either. Since the late 1960s, Sandler Training has interviewed thousands of salespeople about cold calling, as well as many related topics. Those people who professed they liked making cold calls turned out to be the people who *never made any!* The real cold-callers summed up their opinion of cold calling in this visual image: "OK, Christians, the lions are ready!" So much for the professed experts.

SANDLER SELLING TIP

You have to learn to fail to win. When it comes to making cold calls, generating referrals, replying effectively to emails, or doing anything else a professional salesperson must be prepared to do on a daily basis, it's OK to fail. Failure is a part of the human condition. Everybody fails at something. Failure is how we learn. People who achieve a great deal fail at many things. Recognizing failure as a potential positive experience gives you a new freedom: the freedom to try new things, be more creative, and stretch outside your comfort zone.   —DHM

In all fairness, salespeople must assume responsibility for what has happened to our profession, and to us, through the years. We continue to reward the entertainers for their songs and dances. We continue to seek the easy way out, the overnight success, that once-in-a-lifetime seminar that will reveal the secrets to a rich and rewarding career in professional sales. By so doing, we've allowed sales trainers to strip us of our rights and to fill our heads with much that is wrong about the process of selling.

For example, sales trainers have promulgated the idea that it's a salesperson's duty to sell by the numbers. Give presentation after presentation to anyone who will listen, and eventually someone will buy! I'm prepared to tell you that's all wrong. There's no self-esteem in that kind of selling. In fact, it's not selling. It's clerking. And it doesn't work anymore.

Contrary to popular sales training principles, you do not have to give presentations to everyone who will listen to succeed as a salesperson. Nor do you have to perform a dog-and-pony show. You don't have to roll over like a puppy and say that the customer is right. You don't have to be subservient. You don't have to forfeit your self-esteem.

You don't have to fake enthusiasm about your product or service. In fact, *you don't have to be enthusiastic at all!*

And hear this: you don't have to lie.

You can tell your mother and your children that you are a salesperson and never feel embarrassed.

To succeed in sales, you must observe only five rules:

1. Qualify your prospects.
2. Extract your prospect's pain.
3. Verify that the prospect has money.
4. Be sure the prospect is a decision maker.
5. Match your service or product to the prospect's pain.

That's it. Learn these five rules and you'll master the art of professional selling.

When a salesperson and a prospect begin what I call the "selling dance," there are always two systems at work: the prospect's system and the salesperson's system.

In the prospect's system, the agenda is generally one of trying to gather as much information as possible while giving little; negotiating for the best possible price and terms for the goods and services represented; playing the cards close to the vest; and conserving time. There isn't a salesperson alive who wouldn't appreciate the same courtesies. But unfortunately, it rarely happens.

> You can tell your mother and your children that you are a salesperson and never feel embarrassed.

The salespeople I've interviewed through the years have either adopted a traditionally structured selling system or they sell on the fly, not really knowing what they do. For the moment, let's focus on the effectiveness of the salesperson's system (or lack of it) compared to the prospect's system. On balance, our research shows that the prospect usually has the advantage. But it doesn't need to be that way.

Ideally, the salesperson and the prospect should think of selling as a win-win situation. The playing field should be level in sales, but it's not. And that's one of the goals of this book: *to level the playing field so that the salesperson and the prospect can play fairly.*

Clearly, the prospect holds the upper hand today. For years, prospects have considered salespeople as subservient. Salespeople have accepted it, and they continue to do so today. This is evidenced by the many salespeople who spend most of their time waiting to see a buyer. It's similar to the doctor-patient relationship in which doctors who overbook appointments place very little value on their patients' time.

To begin leveling the playing field, every salesperson needs to understand that there are four steps in the prospect's selling system:

1. Prospects don't always tell you the truth, and they play their cards close to the vest. First, you need to understand that in the prospect's value system, it's okay to withhold information from, and even mislead, salespeople. Otherwise honest, upstanding individuals believe they can say anything they want to salespeople.

They do not mislead you because they're bad people; they do so out of a desire for self-preservation. After all, prospects know that while they're busy managing their affairs, you're off attending workshops on how to become a killer salesperson. They know you're learning how to maneuver them into making purchase decisions. And they know your methods work. Each time they choose between meeting a salesperson either Tuesday or Wednesday, in the morning or the afternoon, or at 1 p.m. or 2 p.m., they realize you've done something. They might not be able to identify your technique as the "alternative event close," but they know you've pulled something. And with each new sales encounter, they grow a little bit smarter as your competitors continue to wear out the same collection of time-honored closing techniques.

So how do prospects cope with your superior sales powers? They mislead you. Prospects know one of your first goals is to generate interest in your offering, so they often feign interest in order to pump you for information. The prospect might start off saying, "We've heard wonderful things about your company's ability to . . ." or "We'd like to know how you can help us with . . ." They will tell you the current system is working fine, when in fact, it is in shambles. They will volunteer as little information as possible about their true situation or intentions. They will offer no hint about how much they really need your product or service. They will talk in specific terms about how much money they have to spend. They won't even tell you how to go about making buying decisions. What you must understand as a salesperson is that it doesn't make much difference what your prospect says, because you really can't count on any of it being true.

> If you use traditional selling techniques, you ought to know that your playbook is open to the prospect even before the sales call begins!

Remember, you're not the first salesperson your prospect has encountered. You may be a great, sincere professional with a wonderful opportunity to share. But your prospect doesn't know this. The prospect sees you as "just another salesperson," with all the negative imagery that term implies.

Since World War II, there's been hardly anything new in the profession of traditional sales training. The best traditional sales training gurus lived several generations ago. The teachings of J. Douglas Edwards, Elmer Wheeler, and Charles Roth, to name three of the masters, are simply being rehashed today. But the techniques are old. Today's prospects have grown up with them. They've seen and heard them hundreds, if not thousands, of times.

Too many of today's sales trainers are still touting the old-school curriculum. As a result, they are making salespeople work all the harder. If you use traditional selling techniques, you ought to know that your playbook is open to the prospect even before the sales call begins!

There's even a deeper reason why prospects mislead you. Think about this: Did your mother raise you to go into sales?

Absolutely not! Why not?

Let's think of some words commonly used to describe a salesperson:

Pushy	Liar
Shyster	Offensive
Untrustworthy	Low-life
Polyester snake-oil barker	

What mother would want a child to grow up to be called any of the above? What father would tuck his precious child into bed at night and whisper: "Honey, Daddy wants you to grow up to be a low-life, offensive, untrustworthy liar"?

That's the ugly image that many prospects share today about sales professionals. The general public thinks salespeople are vultures. And prospects don't want to deal with vultures.

What's the easiest way for prospects to defend themselves? Mislead you.

The two most familiar pieces of misdirection sound like this:

- "I'm not interested," when in fact, interest could be generated under more favorable conditions
- "I'm interested," when in fact, the prospect really isn't interested but is afraid of the pressure that might be applied following an honest reply

What you need to understand as a salesperson is that it doesn't matter what prospects say. They reserve the right to mislead you, tell you half-truths (or even smaller fractions of the truth!), and generally throw you off track. If you wait for everyone you talk to about your product or service to volunteer—in plain English, the reality that they don't really want to work with you—you're going to be working way too hard!

SANDLER SELLING TIP

Work smart, not hard. Have you ever held on to a stalled prospect for too long? Have you ever worked really hard to impress someone who either didn't have pain you could remove, didn't have the budget necessary to work with you, or wouldn't share his decision-making process with you? Have you ever projected income from an "opportunity" in which you were doing all the work, and your main contact in the account was doing absolutely nothing? Most of us have been down that road.

Ronald Reagan once said something that works pretty well as advice for professional salespeople facing this problem: "It's true that hard work never killed anyone, but I figure, why take the chance?

It takes two to tango. If you're tangoing all by yourself, you're working too hard. If someone fails to move forward with you on specific, timely, commitment-driven discussions about pain, budget, and decision process, that disqualifies the opportunity. Continuing to chase down an unqualified opportunity may count as hard work, but it is definitely not smart work. It is not a productive use of your time. Too often, we make excuses for working hard in such situations. We may convince ourselves that we "have to" keep going because we've already invested a lot of time, effort, and energy with this person, or because we've gotten a nice, vague email from the contact, or because we feel we have something to prove. These are not smart reasons to go after a piece of business. Disengage and pursue another opportunity that is more viable.   —DHM

You're not the first person who's called on this prospect. And if you're a stranger to the prospect, you're all the more suspect. As a professional, you may not fit the stereotyped image of the despised salesperson, but the amateurs do. They're active. They're attending seminars every day. And they are making sales calls just ahead of you!

2. The prospect wants to know what you know. Why do the prospects like to "pick the brains" of salespeople? Because they know you can help them improve their productivity, lower their costs, and save money. You bring something of value to the marketplace, and if they learn about it, they can improve their own value. The only problem is . . . *they don't want to pay for it!*

Prospects want to extract all you know about your product or service, and they want to negotiate down your best price, just to beat up their existing suppliers. They need to know your numbers so they can say to your competition, "I have a better price than you're giving me." And imagine this: thousands of salespeople in your community are working hard to fulfill this need! As a result, they're corrupting your marketplace.

SANDLER SELLING TIP

Don't try to sell on price alone. David Sandler believed that, in order to avoid being caught in the price trap, professional salespeople must learn to **sell value rather than price.** Yet the vast majority of salespeople still have no idea how to do this, and no interest in learning! (The Sandler Submarine, about which you'll be learning a little later, is the starting point.) The consequences of this perennial sales problem have only increased in the Internet era, when people can compare your stuff with that of the competition just by pulling out their cell phones and typing a few keywords into a browser search box.   —DHM

There's a term for this phenomenon. It's called "unpaid consulting." What's the prognosis for salespeople who don't get paid for what they know? No matter what it is, it can't be good. Just be aware that prospects are engineered to turn you into unpaid consultants. The majority of people who fail in professional selling did a lot of unpaid consulting.

3. The prospect commits to nothing. Prospects who don't get all they're after during the initial sales discussion will ask the salesperson to do a little more work, a little more unpaid consulting. It sounds like this: "I need to think this over." Or, "I'll get back to you." Or, "This is very interesting. I'd like to take this to committee." Or, "We're thinking about putting together a task force to study the feasibility." The prospect holds out just enough hope to make the salesperson believe the chance of a sale exists. That way, the prospect sets up the salesperson for a repeat of step 2 above. I call it the "sucker move."

At the point at which prospects believe they have all they need, or all they're going to get, the process is over. As the salesperson, you're thinking, "Great, I've got another one," when in fact, you probably have nothing.

When prospects want you back again, they "bait" you. Frequently, they use what I call the Humanitarian Public Service Award. It comes in the form of a message like this: "You wrote a great proposal. We got a lot of information out of it. It was of great benefit to us. We would like

to keep abreast of what is going on in our industry, and you have certainly helped us do that. So please keep in touch with us. And by the
way, the gift basket of cookies was very nice. Thank you!"

Why do prospects do this? Simple. It works!

How many times have you seen it work in your marketplace?
Prospects have been using this technique for 2,000 years. They want
your expertise. You do all the work, and then find out nothing is going
to happen. You were misled.

**4. The prospect doesn't answer the telephone and won't return
your messages.** What's really happening? It's over. Only you haven't
been told it's over. And since you've been taught, by the traditional
sales trainers, to follow through and hang in there, you're stuck at the
end of the prospect's system. Of course, it's been over for quite some
time. You couldn't admit it, though, because you invested so much
effort and time chasing what you thought was a real opportunity. It
wasn't.

SANDLER SELLING TIP

You can't lose what you don't have. It shouldn't really come as
a surprise to us that prospects mislead us. All too often, though,
it does. We shouldn't deceive ourselves into believing that we've
qualified a prospect when what's really happened is that we've been
misled, but we haven't yet figured that out. So for instance, assume
someone you spoke to once, briefly, and sent an email message to,
sends you an email in reply. That email says, "Thanks for your call, I'm
really interested in this, I'm looking forward to talking to you." Then,
over a period of weeks, the person never returns your call or makes
any time to talk to you. You're within your rights at some point to
send an email that asks, point-blank, "Hey there. I haven't heard back
from you. Are we done here?" Yet I run into lots of salespeople who
tell me they "can't" send that kind of message. Why not? Because
they're afraid of "losing the opportunity." Losing *what* opportunity?

—DHM

If there's one thing I'm sure of after a lifetime of professional selling, it's this: *if you don't have a selling system of your own when you are with a prospect, you will unknowingly default to the prospect's system.* Why? Because prospects are very good at following their system. You will unknowingly march right down the prospect's path. And nowhere in the prospect's system does it say "sale" or "cash" or "commission check" or "go to the bank." What it does say is: the salesperson loses.

> Business is not won or lost by following the prospect's system. It's won or lost before the prospect's system gets rolling.

The good news is: *you don't have to lose.*

Even better news: you can win the majority of the time if your system is more powerful than your prospect's system! Business is not won or lost by following the prospect's system. It's won or lost before the prospect's system gets rolling and after rapport is established between the salesperson and the prospect.

At that moment of truth, the only question is this: Whose system will prevail? The salesperson's or the prospect's? Your system . . . or their system?

Sandler Training has developed a sales system that's more powerful than the prospect's, and here's how it works:

Step 1. You must uncover your prospect's pain. People buy emotionally, but they make decisions intellectually. What's the most intense emotion? Pain.

Without pain, there's no easy sale. Perhaps there's no sale at all. Without pain, people will continue to do what they've done all their lives until maintaining the status quo becomes so painful that something new is required. Unless you learn to uncover a prospect's pain (which I explain in Chapter 11), you will continue to sell using the most difficult of traditional selling principles: the law of averages!

Remember the second step of the prospect's system? Prospects want you as an unpaid consultant. Don't give them the opportunity! Your mission is to get information ("pain"), not give it.

SANDLER SELLING TIP

Pain. As a professional salesperson, your driving goal is to **identify the gap between where the prospect is and where he or she wants to be.** That gap is something you discover, not something you create. You are not out to cause emotional distress where none existed before.

After all, if this is a real prospect, he or she is *already* concerned, frustrated, unhappy, disappointed, or otherwise emotionally engaged with the existence of that gap between "where I am now" and "where I want to be." Your job is not to create pain but to have good discussions with people that uncover these emotions. One of our specialties is helping you create a customized 30-Second Commercial, which takes the place of the standard features, benefits, and life-story "elevator pitch." Developing this commercial requires one-on-one coaching. You can deploy it not only in face-to-face interactions but also in emails and social media platforms like LinkedIn. It helps you to identify and open discussions with people who have pain gaps that you are likely to be able to fill. For more information on working with a Sandler trainer who can help you develop a customized 30-Second Commercial, visit us at www.sandler.com.   —DHM

Step 2. You must get all the money issues out on the table. While you need to discuss the cost of your product or service, it's more important to discuss the cost to your prospects if they do nothing. Deal with money (see Chapter 12) so that you can get paid for what you do. Once you uncover the prospect's pain and you know money is available to get rid of the pain, you can progress to the third step.

Step 3. You must discover the decision-making process your prospect uses when deciding to buy or not to buy a product or service. Is the prospect empowered to make the decision alone? Will an associate or spouse be involved in the decision making? Does the prospect like to think things over and decide later? Ultimately, can the prospect make the decision to spend the money to get rid of the pain?

Once you're comfortable that you and the prospect clearly understand what it will take to do business together (see Chapter 13), progress to the fourth step.

Step 4. You must present a solution that will get rid of the prospect's pain. Traditionalists would now say, "Aha, this is where you talk features and benefits." No, you don't!

Your sales presentation has little to do with the features and benefits touted by the marketing department and everything to do with showing your prospect that your product or service can eliminate the pain.

Contrary to what the traditionalists say, prospects do not buy features and benefits. They buy things to help them overcome or avoid pain. All you need to do is show your prospects (see Chapter 14) that your product or service will eliminate their pain. It's as simple as that.

Step 5. You must post-sell your sale. How often have your sales slipped away after you've concluded the sale? Perhaps it doesn't happen in your business. But when a salesperson takes business away from a competitor, the competitor usually doesn't surrender. Has your competitor ever sent you a congratulatory note that says, "Nice going, George! Good luck with your new client"?

Chances are, the competitor will make a run at saving the business. How? By lowballing your price. Once the gloves are off, the competitor isn't going to be pleasant about it.

Without a Post-Sell step (see Chapter 15), you may get assaulted by your competitor. A strong and effective Post-Sell step will prevent your new customer from contacting you to say, "Please call. We need to talk." Or, "Hold up temporarily. I've run into a problem."

By following this five-step system, which is currently used successfully by countless sales professionals around the world, you can expect to win the selling dance the majority of the time.

If your present selling cycle is to follow the prospect's path, and now you understand what's happening to you, what can you do? Not much. For the moment, relax. But promise yourself it will never happen again. Consider it a part of your *new* sales education.

If you make the same mistake again, by the way, we have a term for that. It's called "being at the Wimp Junction®." You're wimping out on your goals, your income, your family, and your future. Wimps are people without self-esteem. They're the puppy dogs of the sales profession. Prospects belittle them. And they rarely win. They're like the kids who never give up their training wheels or who never get back on the bike after falling off. I doubt you're one of them, or you wouldn't be reading this book.

By this time you might be wondering: Who is this Sandler? And more important: What gives him the right to think he knows so much about mastering the art of professional selling?

If you'll continue reading, I'll explain everything to you, including a system that will help you master the art of professional selling.

2

WHAT I DID AFTER THE COOKIE CRUMBLED

When I'm scared, I'll drive myself to do

whatever's necessary to get the job done.

—**DAVID H. SANDLER**

I was 36 years old and on "easy street" when I lost a job that should have lasted all of my life. It was, after all, my family's business, and I had inherited it at the age of 27. But suddenly, on a Friday afternoon in March 1967, with a family, two company cars, a country club membership, a boat, a mortgage, and no money in the bank, I lost a proxy fight with my business partner, and I was out of a job.

It was the most frightening experience of my life. I had never been without a paycheck.

My father had made a business selling snacks: cookies, crackers, potato chips, and pretzels. As a youngster, I spent my summers working in the business, but I didn't go to work full-time until I returned from the Korean War in 1953. I started as a route driver calling on small grocery stores. Two years later, my father died, and I took control of the business.

By 1960, I was rapidly expanding the business between Baltimore and Philadelphia, and I needed capital. One of my suppliers was willing to back me financially, so I formed a corporate partnership with him. Unfortunately, my lawyer failed to explain to me that my partner controlled the voting shares of stock in the company, and he had the right to fire me. That was the beginning of the end. For six years, the business prospered, and I couldn't have been happier. I remember, in fact, a glorious spring afternoon in 1966. I was at the country club, walking along a path lined with colorful flowers, and savoring the smell of the freshly cut grass. I was an avid golfer, and there was nothing more beautiful to me than a meticulously groomed golf course. I remember looking around and thinking how lucky I was. At the age of 35, I was essentially retired. I had it made! Except that I couldn't see what was about to happen to me. As the famous American newscaster

John Chancellor said after he retired from broadcasting and discovered that he had cancer: "If you want to make God laugh, tell him your plans."

My partner wasn't a golfer, and he didn't appreciate the time I spent at the country club. He was busy running his own manufacturing business, so one Friday afternoon he sent a guy to tell me that I was fired. Just like that. One minute, I was making a very nice salary, with lots of perks, and the next minute it was gone.

Monday morning, some people came to my home and drove away my company cars. I didn't have any money, so I had to forfeit my country club membership and sell my boat. I was humiliated, not to mention scared and angry. Mostly, I was angry, and, of course, that led to a feeling of revenge. I told my former partner he had no right to *my* business. Then I vowed to get him. I told him I would put him out of business; I even predicted the date that it would happen.

I then did a stupid thing. I spent the next eight months taking away a good part of the business and giving it to a former competitor. I put my business out of business! It wasn't hard to do. I joined a competitor, and one by one I took away my former partner's customers. They were all my accounts anyway.

I had read about the power of visualization, so I put up a bankruptcy poster board in my bedroom, and every night and every morning I looked at it and said, "I'm going to get you," referring, of course, to my former partner. I picked the day, and then I devoted all my energy to that senseless, emotional goal. Today, we'd call it a Dream Board, but it was really a negative Dream Board, dedicated to the goal of destroying something. I don't recommend that, by the way.

SANDLER SELLING TIP

The road to success is always under construction. Lots of people's lives—mine, for instance—would have been very different indeed if David Sandler hadn't moved past his initial Dream Board and found something newer and better to visualize. One of the most important ways we serve our clients is by helping them revise and update the goals they've set for themselves and their organizations, so that those goals are viable, just challenging enough, consistent with one another, and in alignment with all the relevant values. We find that most of the new people we work with haven't yet put their current goals in writing. That's an essential first step, although, as the story here suggests, you can and should think twice about written goals that don't actually support you.   —DHM

On the very day that I had predicted, I put him out of business. I even went back and bought my old desk. But I had wasted all that time and energy. The best thing he ever did was fire me.

Getting fired forced me to explore job opportunities that I would otherwise never have considered. A classified ad in the Baltimore newspaper led me to the sales profession. It was something to do, part-time, until I could rebuild my business. Or at least, so I thought. As it turned out, I never left professional sales. In fact, after a few initial years of trial and error in sales, I developed my own sales training program and founded Sandler Training. Today, the Sandler Selling System® is used coast to coast by tens of thousands of businesses and sales professionals, and it's taught by more than 200 franchisees who have been certified by our company. There isn't another profession that would have afforded me the opportunity to make an impact on so many lives and businesses. And it all happened because of a disgruntled partner who just didn't like the fact that I could run a business and have plenty of time to play golf too.

Of course, at the time I was fired, I didn't see things this clearly. If you've ever lost a job, you know what I mean. However, I'm a guy who believes that when one door closes, somewhere another door opens. But in the midst of the turmoil that follows the loss of a job, especially when you didn't see it coming, who can think clearly? When you're down and out, and you're worried about how you'll support your family and what you'll say to your friends and neighbors, it's a stretch of faith to believe that everything will not only be OK *but better*.

It took some time for me to think clearly, especially while I was preoccupied with revenge. All I knew was that I had to replace $30,000 a year (which was a lot in 1967 dollars), plus the perks. At that time, working with the competition, I was earning only $12,500. Instead of my Buick Riviera, equipped with one of the first AT&T car phones, I was now driving a 1966 Volkswagen without air-conditioning. If life was going to get better, I figured it wasn't going to be in the snack business.

A distributor of motivational materials—audios and workbooks—ran the help-wanted ad in the *Baltimore Sun* that caught my attention. I answered the ad because it was work I could do at night to supplement my income. I had never sold anything like "motivation" before. In the snack business, there wasn't much selling. If you took care of your accounts, you kept them forever. Selling a package of motivational materials was foreign to me, but I figured I could learn how to do it. Besides, the distributor had a training program that would supposedly ensure my success. For three weeks at night, I sat in the distributor's basement watching training films and reading a workbook that taught me the principles of traditional selling.

I learned how to make a sales presentation, what to say, and when to say it. I learned how to use different selling and closing techniques, as well as when to hiccup, when to pause, and when to stop talking. The training was tedious, but I was now smart enough to know that if someone gave me a system that worked, I should follow it!

I studied the training materials enthusiastically. I was fascinated by the recorded messages of Napoleon Hill and Earl Nightingale, and for the first time in my life, I learned about goal setting. Every night I reported to the distributor's basement office at five o'clock and stayed until ten or eleven. I continued listening to the recordings even when I got home. My first goal was to absorb the material and memorize the presentation word for word until I could repeat it flawlessly. At the time, I thought this was what selling was all about, and I was determined to master the system. I wasn't a kid anymore trying to be creative.

At the end of the third week of training, it was finally time to go out and sell. That meant I had to cold call relatives and friends and eventually any stranger who would listen to me. The ideal sales call involved delivering the presentation, going for the close, handling stalls and objections, and getting the order, all in one session. My package sold for $400, and along with the motivational materials, it included a portable record player and batteries!

Nights and weekends, I called on anyone who would listen to me about buying my product, which promised to turn him or her into a better person. I had a $30,000 nut to crack with only $12,500 of income from my daytime job, so money was my motivation. Almost immediately I made a few sales, for which I earned a commission. But in that same short period of time, I discovered this was a crazy business, and I hated it!

In the food industry, if a customer tells you to ship him a trailer of fig bars, he pays you, and you ship the fig bars. But in the business of traditional selling, you make a presentation and a prospect says, "Come back on Monday and I'll give you a check for $400." And on Monday you can't find him. Or he won't see you.

I didn't (and I don't) understand that kind of business. It's not a business that's worthy of my time. All the salespeople whom my distributor recruited must have thought so, too, because they all quit. They just disappeared. But I didn't. It wasn't that I didn't want to. I was stuck. I had no choice. *I needed the money.* Every time I thought selling was too tough and demanding or that the business was a waste of my time, I forced myself to continue trying because *I needed the money.*

Everything about the traditional selling process was painful for me. I hated starting from scratch every time with a new presentation. I didn't like feeling the pressure, then applying the pressure to the prospect, and still not knowing the outcome. Would I get the sale or not? Earn a commission or not? I hated being enthusiastic when I really wasn't. And worst of all, I hated doing all the talking.

In spite of all my reluctance, I managed to make three to four sales a month on a part-time basis. And that meant I was bringing in an additional $10,000 to $12,000 a year.

I learned a lot about traditional selling during this process, but I also learned a lot about myself. I discovered that I didn't like small talk. I didn't know how to do it. I was an only child for 13 years, so I wasn't outgoing or expressive. It was neither easy nor comfortable for me to interact with people. I was no social animal. To some people that meant I could not succeed at sales.

SANDLER SELLING TIP

Even introverts can become great salespeople. As David Sandler's life story proves, and as tens of thousands of our graduates can attest, introverts can and do destroy quota. Even someone who loathes small talk, is not outgoing, and doesn't particularly enjoy interacting with strangers can create a career as a superior sales performer. If anyone ever tells you that you have to have the "gift of gab" and love meeting total strangers in order to succeed in sales, have that person call us.   —DHM

Furthermore, I didn't know what to talk *about*. I wasn't comfortable talking about money because that wasn't a subject we discussed in my family. I wasn't comfortable doing a dog-and-pony show about my product. And I didn't know how to lead people to make decisions because that wasn't something I had ever had to do. Under these circumstances, you can assume it wasn't easy to keep a positive mental attitude. I was scared! I had no money, and the future didn't look promising.

It was only the fear that I wouldn't be able to pay my bills that forced me to continue selling, and it was a constant struggle. On one occasion, unbelievable to me now, I drove past a wholesale restaurant equipment showroom while thinking to myself, "That looks like a good business that would be a good prospect for my product." Instead of stopping, I pushed harder on the accelerator and continued driving! Six blocks later, my head caught up with my foot, and I turned the car around. "Why would I just drive by that business?" I asked myself.

Of course, the answer is obvious. I didn't want to experience the pain of the cold call all over again. I didn't want to feel the pressure. Most of all, I didn't want to be rejected again. But I made a U-turn that day, and I went back and called on that business. And as fate would have it, I had attended high school with the owner of the business. The U-turn resulted in a $1,500 commission!

Back in my car, where I made it a habit to analyze my sales calls, I thought it was interesting that I had to fight with myself to turn the car around to make a sales call that put money in my pocket. With that one sale, I had earned more money in less than an hour than I could earn in a month at my daytime job. I could get used to that! And yet, I almost didn't make the call. Suddenly as painful as selling was most of the time for me, the *opportunity* to make a big commission was motivation enough to keep me interested in the business.

One day, for reasons that I can't explain, I arrived at a turning point in my life. I was sitting in my car at an intersection waiting for the light to change, and I remember thinking that I could turn left and make another cold call, or I could turn right and go back to my distributor's office. I turned right.

The distributor was a man who sat behind a desk and collected the money. He never made a sales call, and he had no intention of ever doing so. By now, I was his only sales-person, and he benefited by my hard work. I got to thinking, "Why do I need him?" I went to his office, and I said, "Stan, I'm leaving you."

> I arrived at a turning point in my life.

"You can't," he said. "You're the only person selling anything! I need you."

"Well, I don't think there's a future in this business for me," I explained.

I could see the panic in Stan's eyes as we talked for the next half hour. I provided the only living that he was making, and without me he would have to close the business. Finally I said, "Stan, I'll tell you what. I'll buy all your materials, and your distributorship, for 20 cents on the dollar." That came to $2,500. Stan thought for a moment and asked me to come back the next day.

Stan must have sharpened his pencil overnight, and admitting to himself that he wasn't going to sell anything on his own, he decided my offer made sense. "You've got a deal," he told me the next day, a Sunday. Just like that I became a distributor of motivational audio recordings and books. But now I had an even bigger decision to make.

Later that day, I found myself sitting on the side of the road trying to work up the nerve to quit my daytime job. I thought about a message that I had heard from Earl Nightingale, whose recordings were part of my motivational package. In *The Strangest Secret*, Nightingale said I could be anything I wanted to be. He said that 95 percent of people are followers. They have no interest in accomplishing anything new, but they are willing to follow someone else. What a huge market for a guy selling a motivational program!

To accomplish something new, however, I would have to give up what I had. That meant giving up $12,500 annually, and the Volkswagen, which was better than no car at all. It meant forfeiting a paycheck, buying a car, and then, at 36 years of age, trying to succeed again on my own. I didn't know how I could succeed *and* work full-time at another job. I didn't want to give up the security I had. But then again, to succeed in selling, I'd have to devote myself to the profession. Success would be worth it. I figured out that if I set two appointments per day, I could net three to five sales a week. The profits would add up to more money than I had been making with two jobs! *That* motivated me. I didn't like selling, but I liked collecting money. And I had already proven that I could do it, in spite of my distaste for the business.

Finally, I talked myself into it. Monday morning, I resigned from the snack business, never to return. Now I was back in business for myself, full-time, selling motivational materials with some distant support from a home office in Texas.

It didn't take long to set up a desk at home, in a room next to my bedroom, and get to work. I grabbed the Yellow Pages and started dialing the telephone. I had learned in my traditional sales training not to predetermine whom to call. The idea was to just barrel forward and get myself in front of people! So I decided to cold call any business that looked like a prospect.

I soon discovered how much I hated cold calling. I'm sure I was more reluctant than anyone else who has ever made a cold call. Every time I picked up the phone, I cringed. Like most salespeople, I have a high need to be accepted, and since most cold calls result in rejection, I got sick to my stomach before every call. When I woke up in the morning, if I knew I had to make cold calls that day, my stomach churned.

How I Overcame Call Reluctance on the Telephone

In the early days of my sales career, I had to trap myself into doing things that I found uncomfortable. Cold calling by phone was one of those things, and here's the trap that I created to cure my reluctance.

Anytime I called on a sales manager, I offered a free, valuable service. I said:

"If you will allow me to visit your next sales meeting, I will give your people some tips about how to overcome call reluctance on the telephone. I'm sure they'll find it worthwhile. If you're impressed by my information, then all I ask is that you give me an appointment to talk to you about what I might do for your people as their sales trainer."

The sales manager accepted my offer 9 out of 10 times.

I'd then go to an insurance company or a real estate office and stand up in front of the room and talk for a few minutes about call reluctance. I explained that most salespeople despised cold calling. I got everyone to agree with me that cold calling was the most unpleasant experience that we had to face in our sales careers. Then I'd reverse the situation and say, "Here, let me show you how easy it is to cold call on the telephone."

I'd ask a member of the sales team to get a copy of the Yellow Pages. Then I said, "Open the book to any category you like. The category doesn't make any difference." They'd pick funeral directors, lumberyards, and so on. I'd go to the telephone and make a cold call to whatever business they selected for me. This was a *real* cold call. They thought I was making the cold call for them, but I was doing it for *me!*

For half an hour or so, I'd make cold calls in front of this audience, all the while demonstrating the elements that worked. In between calls, I provided live analysis peppered with my own sense of humor. Usually, by the time I finished, I had set two or three appointments for myself! Later, I called on those prospects.

This was a better performance than I could turn in at home. In front of an audience, my adrenaline started pumping. I became more fluid, more assertive. I said things I might not say at home or sitting alone, behind my desk. For my own good, I forced myself into this trap at least once a week.

Of course, I also sold the sales manager my motivational package because he couldn't believe that someone would come into his sales meeting, pick up a telephone, make cold calls, and book appointments. His people always picked up something from the exercise, so he immediately saw the benefit of my training.

The real value of this trap, however, was that I made appointments for myself. I turned cold calling into an exercise that was challenging and fun. When you trap yourself like this, it doesn't take long to become proficient at whatever it is you're trying to accomplish.

One morning, I had made 20 or so calls, and my wife, Edna, walked behind me, put her hand on my shoulder, and said, "Do you know your shirt is soaking wet?" I hadn't realized it, but I perspired profusely while making cold calls. It was a traumatic experience for me. I didn't know what I wanted more—to actually reach someone on the phone or to hear a busy signal, which meant I wouldn't have to talk and I wouldn't get rejected.

At the same time, I was feeling the pressure of running my own business. I didn't have a paycheck. I was all alone. And I didn't want to fail. I was scared. The good thing is that when I'm scared, I'll drive myself to do whatever's necessary to get the job done. So that meant I had to make cold calls. Traditional sales training told me I had to get myself in front of enough people every week to make sales. Even so, cold calling was going to give me a heart attack!

SANDLER SELLING TIP

Leverage your LinkedIn connections. No matter how advanced the communication technology gets, sales professionals are still going to need to reach out to new people. The trick is to pick the technology that makes that easy to do. These days, one of the best ways to warm up your cold calling is to use your LinkedIn network effectively. (By the way, if you're not on LinkedIn, you should be.) Let's assume Juan Delgado is a first-degree contact of yours, and let's assume that you see that he's directly connected on LinkedIn to Angela Yee, to whom you want to be connected. What do you do? You send Juan an email—preferably not a LinkedIn message, since those are more likely to be ignored. Your email says: "Hey there, Juan, I happened to notice on your LinkedIn profile that you're connected to Angela Yee over at ABC Company. How well do you know her? Would you be willing to introduce me?"

In most cases, Juan will reply by saying something along these lines: "Sure, I know Angela. I'd be happy to introduce you." You then send a reply to Juan that says, "Juan, I got your message. Thank you so much for that. My experience is that an email introduction can work very well for everyone involved. I have attached a template for your review. Please feel free to edit it in any way you want." The template you attach will briefly and plausibly introduce you as a potential resource for Angela, and then it suggests that Angela reach out to you.

Most of the time, Juan approves this template, and he simply sends out your message, unedited, to Angela, copying you on the correspondence. Immediately thereafter, you email both Juan and Angela with this: "Hey, Juan. Thanks so much for the introduction. Angela, I'm really looking forward to speaking with you. I'm out of the office on Monday, Tuesday, and Wednesday of this week, but I will be back in on Thursday. I will reach out to you by phone then. What's the best number to use?" You've just set up a phone appointment!
                                                            —DHM

The Not-Enough-Money-in-Your-Pocket Trap

One morning, knowing that I only had $2 in my pocket, I purposely parked my car at a lot in downtown Baltimore.

It was a trap because I would need $5 to get the car back! (This was before the rise of ATMs.) Consequently, if I planned to eat lunch that day and drive my car home that night, I'd have to stay on the street making cold calls until I collected some cash.

This turned out to be an exercise in motivation for the day because whenever I sat down to think about quitting, I had to keep going. The only possible way I could collect any money was to continue making cold calls. Sooner or later, if I made enough cold calls, I figured I was bound to be successful.

At four o'clock in the afternoon, my pocket was empty. I had spent the $2 on lunch. But now I was calling on a mortgage company. I made my usual presentation. And bingo! The prospect liked my product, and he agreed to buy. I told him that I would return the next day to deliver the product. Meanwhile, I asked my new customer for a small deposit. That's when he grabbed his checkbook, but I stopped him. "Wait a minute. Rather than a check, can you give me cash?" He had $10 in his pocket. I said, "That's fine. Just give me the $10, and you can pay me the balance tomorrow."

I didn't bother to tell him why I needed the cash, but I was sure happy to get it!

Anyone who says he likes cold calling never made many cold calls, in my opinion. I can't imagine feeling comfortable calling strangers, trying to talk your way past the gatekeeper, talking to people who don't really want to talk to you, jumping up and down enthusiastically about your product, and spending so much effort on people you wouldn't normally spend 10 minutes with at a social event. But if you're selling a product or service that doesn't easily lend itself to lead generation, there's nothing to do but cold call. Or so I thought at the time. Later, I would figure out a better way!

The Three-Foot-Rule Trap

Since I wasn't a social animal, and I didn't like approaching strangers, I created a trap that forced me to talk to strangers. I promised myself that whenever I was in public, if I got within three feet of someone who looked like a prospect for my product, I would say, "What do you do for a living?" If I could reach out and touch someone, whether I liked it or not, I had to use the Three-Foot Rule.

Most of the time, this trap didn't result in a sale, but it helped me overcome my reluctance to talk to strangers. And as it turned out, it only had to work once to make it worthwhile. One day I was in an elevator, and before the door closed, an elderly man joined me. I could have reached over and touched him so I said, "What do you do for a living?"

He said he worked for a finance company, and as the elevator continued climbing floors, I told him about my product. Somehow, I got myself invited to his home that evening.

That night, I found myself sitting in this man's living room with his aged mother and father, who didn't have a clue why I was there. It turned out that my prospect was a Civil War buff, and for two hours I heard about his trips to Kentucky and West Virginia, and the history of the Civil War.

Finally, I got the opportunity to make my presentation, and I made the sale. He asked me to deliver the product to him the next day at his office in downtown Baltimore, and he would give me a check.

The next morning, I found my new client at his office dressed in a suit and fashionable tie with a stick pin. He welcomed me, gave me a check for $400, and then he offered to introduce me to the company president.

It's what happened next that made all my Three-Foot-Rule experiences worthwhile! The company president asked me to give him a presentation, and when I finished, he handed me a second check. This one was for $6,000! It was the first time I had ever made a multiple sale to the same customer. The president decided to buy motivational packages for his entire sales staff.

My friend from the elevator subsequently introduced me to one of his clients, who owned one of Baltimore's largest breweries. The result was several more thousand dollars of income and an introduction to one of Baltimore's best-known car dealers.

The car dealer invited me to speak to Baltimore's Forty Thieves, an association of used-car dealers who met at the local Holiday Inn. About 30 car dealers heard my presentation, and I eventually sold my product to all of them. These sales occurred all because I asked one stranger in an elevator, "What do you do for a living?"

As awkward as it was to use this trap, I discovered one thing: it sure beat cold calling! The process taught me that the best way to get in front of a prospect is via an introduction from an existing customer. In other words, spend time to get referrals.

I soon realized that cold calling by phone all day wasn't going to help me earn enough money. Sometimes, at the end of a long day, I had nothing to show for my efforts. Maybe a few appointments, if that. So I decided to change my strategy. I worked the phone only until 10 a.m., and then I left the house to call on my appointments and to cold call in between the appointments. I told Edna to lock the doors and not let me back in the house until 6 p.m.

Cold calling wasn't my only avenue to appointments. My distributorship's home office occasionally sent me leads, or at least what they believed were leads. One of my first live presentations was the result of a lead from Texas. This particular lead was from a man in Delaware, which was about a two-and-a-half-hour drive from my home. I contacted the man by phone, set up an appointment, packed my records and portable record player, and drove over the Chesapeake Bay Bridge into Delaware.

I knocked on the door of a farmhouse, and a gentleman wearing a T-shirt and carrying a shaggy old dog answered the door. The old farmer invited me in, and I spent the next 45 minutes delivering a flawless presentation about my motivational materials, just as I had been taught. Finally, I got down to the close. All this time, the old guy hadn't said a word, but he listened intently, occasionally stroking the back of his dog. It wasn't until I was finished that he looked at me and said, "I don't have any money."

I got back in my car and drove two and a half hours back to Baltimore. "There's got to be something wrong," I said to myself as I headed home. I had been taught to give a presentation to anyone who would listen to me. But I had spent the entire day chasing a lead for absolutely no return. I had been taught to do all the talking. And this time—as was true most of the time—it didn't pay off. My training had taught me to sell features and benefits and to create curiosity. Then, I was supposed to close the sale and collect the money. I did everything perfectly too. But I had absolutely nothing to show for my time or my talent.

It was on that day, driving back to Baltimore, that I began developing my own selling system. Having been trapped by traditional selling, I was about to spring myself free. In Nightingale's recording of *The Strangest Secret*, he said that anyone who's willing to spend five years to learn a profession could eventually get people to line up to pay him for what he knew. And that's what I decided to do. That day in the car, I committed myself to the profession of selling. For five years, for better or worse, I would immerse myself in sales training. I accepted Nightingale's premise. I believed people would line up to pay me large sums of money for my expertise.

And they have!

Now, in the chapters that follow, I'm about to share it all with you.

SANDLER SELLING TIP

Invest in LinkedIn's Sales Navigator Tool. Before we leave the topic of prospecting, I want to share a few more insights about LinkedIn, and specifically the Sales Navigator Tool. This subscription-based application (not to be confused with LinkedIn's free offerings) allows you to leverage the LinkedIn connections of others who work for your company, dramatically broadening your personal networking landscape. It also generates tailored lead recommendations based on criteria you set, tracks current opportunities, gives you timely and accurate updates about your active prospects, and lets you create a professional, trusted brand with a premium profile. As if all that weren't enough, it syncs up with your CRM Tool. For more information, visit http://sales.linkedin.com/blog/the-social-selling-era-starts-now/.   —DHM

3

THE EVOLUTION OF A TRAINING PROGRAM THAT WILL TEACH YOU TO SUCCEED IN SALES

If the competition is doing it, stop it

right away. Do something else!

—DAVID H. SANDLER

It took a long time for me to realize that traditional selling was all wrong and that it didn't work. Who was I, after all, to make such a pronouncement? There were thousands of successful salespeople in the United States using traditional selling techniques. If the techniques didn't work for me, it would have seemed right to conclude that there was something wrong with *me*.

But I didn't think so. I had demonstrated that I could master the traditional selling techniques, beginning with what the trainers called "spaced repetition," in which I listened to the same tapes over and over until I knew the scripts verbatim. I talked to myself approvingly, wrote positive thoughts on three-by-five cards, and repeated the thoughts every day. I believed these exercises would make a difference in my life, and, in fact, I know even today that these methods work—to a degree. But for what purpose? No, the problem wasn't me or my ability. The problem was, traditional selling just didn't feel right.

I could sell features and benefits, arouse interest and curiosity, and close sales, as evidenced by the commissions I earned. Sure, I could make a $1,500 sale in less than an hour, but it took me three days of torture to do it, and another three days to repeat it. Traditional selling was painful, and I hated it. I was working too hard for too little reward, as were the other salespeople I knew. What price were the traditional sales trainers expecting us to pay for success? Frankly, there were much easier ways to make a living.

One rainy afternoon, immediately following that fateful trip to Delaware in the late 1960s, I was sitting in a Dunkin' Donuts. My feet were wet, my clothing was damp, and I said to myself: "This is crazy. I'm going from building to building making cold calls, and I'm not getting results. If there's a better way to sell, what is it?"

My mind was willing to believe that there must be a better way, but I was stuck trying to come up with it. Much later, I learned how to charge through this thought process and short-circuit the emotional turmoil. I simply created a rule that I use to this day: *If the competition is doing it, stop it right away. Do something else!* It doesn't matter what else. Just do something else.

As I concentrated on my personal quest to understand how to succeed in sales and to find a different way to sell, I read everything I could about sales training, and also about human dynamics. I wasn't a machine. I had feelings and emotions, ups and downs, good and bad days, just like everyone else. The little child inside of me triggered the notion that my ability to sell might not be solely mechanical. It might be related to my personality. So I read books about human dynamics.

It just so happened that my search for knowledge coincided with the transactional analysis (TA) trend of the late 1960s. TA is a psychological theory that analyzes the structure of social interactions, and I thought it could be applied to sales. Eric Berne, the author of *Games People Play*, originated the theory, and Thomas A. Harris popularized it with his book *I'm OK—You're OK* in 1969.

About this time, I was asking myself questions like these: "How did I end up in a sales career?" "Was I supposed to buy this distributorship?" "Why did I get fired from the snack business?" "Why don't I have enough money?" "Aren't I supposed to be on 'easy street' by now?" "Is there someone or something to blame for all of this?"

The books I read helped convince me that I was responsible for *all* of it. Whatever happened, I had done it to myself. One day I said, "Sandler, you put yourself here. Nobody did anything to you. You're here because you are."

SANDLER TRAINING TIP

When your foot hurts, you're probably standing on your own toe. Whether or not salespeople like to admit it, there is no point trying to blame the prospect—or the economy, or your manager, or your computer system—for problems that arise during the sales process. When you get right down to it, there are really only two things that can go wrong when you are in discussions with a prospective buyer: either you said or did something you weren't supposed to . . . or you *didn't* say or do something you *were* supposed to. Either way, you can figure out who was responsible by consulting the nearest mirror. Blaming anyone else is like standing on your own toe, then looking around for the person who made your foot hurt.   —DHM

TA revolutionized my thinking about my role as a salesperson. I became so interested in TA that Edna and I traveled to Berkeley, California, the home of TA, to study more about it, but we found nothing there that I couldn't buy in a bookstore at home. I was fascinated to learn about my alternate personality states, which TA described as the "Parent," "Adult," and "Child," and to see how these personalities could disrupt my life. I was equally fascinated to learn how I could improve my life by updating my Adult ego state to override the Parent and Child states that conditioned my behavior beginning in my childhood. By making behavioral changes, I began to realize that I could dramatically change my life over a period of time. I didn't fully comprehend how it would work at the time, but I knew it was much deeper than using motivational one-liners to attempt to effect change.

I could easily accept the TA theory that human lives are structured as scripts, or life plans for obtaining certain payoffs or goals. And that people repeatedly play certain games by which they elicit psychological payoffs. TA taught us that people frequently do what they have to do because they're driven to it by childhood.

Most significantly to me, TA promoted the theory that people need a minimum level of social gratification, or "strokes." We need to be accepted. For anyone in sales, the need for acceptance creates enormous conflict. How do you find acceptance in a profession that's filled with rejection? The answer that had been eluding me was now within my grasp.

Why Salespeople Don't Take Risks

Traditional sales training does not differentiate between "identity" and "role." Proponents of traditional sales training simply teach the material, sometimes in a very entertaining format, but they place the responsibility for using the material on the salesperson.

So what happens? The salesperson sits at home, stuck with personal flaws related to identity, and he can't perform. He takes no risks. Not being able to use what he has learned simply makes him feel worse. He gets caught in a downward spiral of failure and rejection. He continues to find himself not doing what he's supposed to do—for example, not leaving his home to make sales calls. Pressure, guilt, self-doubt, worry, and fear will eventually totally immobilize this salesperson.

The Sandler Selling System separates identity and role. And by doing so, we reduce the risk factors in a salesperson's life. Since self-esteem cannot be hurt by the rejection of the sales process, a salesperson will continually take risks ... more risks, and higher risks, leading to bigger sales.

The Sandler Selling System doesn't merely teach techniques and strategies. Human relations skills are included as well. The result is that salespeople whom we train are able to use the techniques and strategies with ease and success.

Why "10s" Continue to Grow

When I tell people their identity is always a 10, some of them argue that it's impossible because a rating of 10 implies they have no room to grow. They say, "If I was 10 when I was born, and 10 when I was 11 and 25, and I'm a 10 today, then how did I grow?"

OK, imagine that you are going to plant a seed in the ground. The seed is going to grow into a rose. When you plant the seed, what's the value of the seed and everything in it? Can we agree that it's a 10?

Now, after a couple of weeks of sunshine and water, a stem wiggles up from out of the seed and appears above ground. What's the value of that stem? Can it be anything other than a 10? If you say it's less than a 10, then explain when it lost value. It didn't, of course!

So after 6 weeks, what's the value of the rose? In 15 weeks, what's the value of the rose? It continues to be a 10. So the rose was a 10 as a seed, and it's a 10 now. And yet, didn't it grow?

Just because your identity is valued at a 10 doesn't mean you stopped growing. You grow all the time.

However, that's not to say you don't have psychological trash. In fact, everyone does! It's part of being human. If you were the only person with psychological trash, then you'd have a problem. But we've all got some of it, and in spite of it, we continue to be 10s, and we continue to grow.

While I was not a psychologist, TA made sense to me as both a layman and a sales professional. I found in TA various explanations for the problems that I was encountering as an apprentice salesperson. Not long after reading *I'm OK—You're OK* and *Games People Play*, I got the opportunity to use TA in my field. One of my clients, who was the chairman of a large national company, called me and said, "Sandler, I like your training materials, and now I need your help. We've got 20 administrative assistants who report to the vice presidents in our organization, and I need you to teach them something about how to get along better among themselves."

By building on my frequent visits to sales meetings to teach people how to overcome call reluctance, I had expanded into sales training. However, I had nothing to say to administrative assistants, or to anyone, for that matter, who wasn't interested in learning how to sell. Furthermore, I had no qualifications for teaching people how to get along better. But I couldn't say no to this client. He wasn't asking me to help him. He *expected* me to help him. So I decided to build a course using the TA material. It was all about how to get along with people.

I created a seminar for the assistants in which I demonstrated the Parent, Adult, Child theories of transactional analysis. I developed scenarios in which one assistant's Child state clashed with another administrative assistant's Critical Parent state, and then I talked about some of the games that people played to counterbalance the effects of such behavior. The four hours turned out to be informative and fun, and I went away feeling good about the experience. I didn't know if it would help matters or not, but I had delivered what my client had asked me to do. I expected nothing else to come out of it.

> I want you to come back and teach the same seminar to our 200 salespeople.

A week later, my client called and said, "I don't know what you did for these employees, but their attitudes have changed. They're getting along better. Everyone feels better as a result of your seminar. I want you to come back and teach the same seminar to our 200 salespeople."

SANDLER TRAINING TIP

Sandler is a way to transform your life that happens to also transform your sales performance. As the story of the administrative assistants suggests, the Sandler methodology can and does transform whole organizations, not just sales teams. It has also been known to transform family relationships. (See also the case studies in Appendix A at the end of the book.)   —DHM

Now I was worried. This wasn't *my* material! I didn't see any problem teaching one short seminar using what I knew about transactional analysis, but if word got around that some sales trainer in Baltimore was making a profit using TA theories that didn't belong to him, would I end up getting sued? I wanted someone to give me the approval to use the TA material, but as it turned out, TA was in the public domain. I was free to do with the information whatever I wished. I could teach the seminar, and no one would care. When I presented the TA seminar to the salespeople, I analyzed the anatomy of various sales. At the point that I said, "The Child wants to buy, the Adult makes the decision, and the Parent gives permission to the Child to have what the Adult wants," it began to sound like magic. Everyone, including me, was focused on the human dynamics issues of professional selling. At the time, traditional sales trainers taught nothing about self-awareness. Most still don't!

When I wasn't teaching seminars, I continued making my own sales calls to build my business. Now, however, I

> The Child wants to buy, the Adult makes the decision, and the Parent gives permission to the Child to have what the Adult wants.

began experimenting with the ideas that I had learned from my study of transactional analysis. I became much more aware of myself in the sales process. I started to recognize the Not-OK little person inside of me who needed approval—the same approval that all salespeople require.

I discovered that it was better to leave the little guy behind in the car when I called on a prospect. This Child was six years old and afraid to take a risk. He could never go into a sales call prepared to lay his cards on the table. He would rather sacrifice his self-esteem than take a chance. He was afraid to fail, or to arouse his Critical Parent, who would scold him if he failed.

> The only person in my psyche who wasn't afraid to take risks was my Adult.

The only person in my psyche who wasn't afraid to take risks was my Adult. He knew that the most a prospect could say was no. He wasn't afraid of trial and error. Unlike the Child, he didn't live or die by someone's approval. Therefore, he never had to fake. My Adult didn't have to act out some scenario in front of a prospect and then blame his failure on something else if he didn't make a sale. He didn't have to sacrifice his self-esteem. He could say it straight and not be manipulative. My Adult didn't have to play Willie Loman!

And so I left my Child and my Critical Parent roles behind me, and I called on prospects with my Adult and my Nurturing Parent to support me. Together, we made up a human relations model that allowed me to fail sometimes, and to win sometimes, but to feel good about myself all the time. That's what traditional salespeople can't do even today. They have to sacrifice feeling good about themselves because, in their minds, selling is a win-lose proposition. Someone always wins, and someone always loses. When they sell, they win; when they don't, they lose. I was soon to discover that's all wrong. Selling can always be a win-win proposition.

I didn't clearly understand all of this while I was in the midst of my trial-and-error period, which began in the late 1960s and continued during the early years of the 1970s. But as I began to develop my own selling system, I had learned enough from TA to value the psychology of human dynamics in professional selling. No one had ever done that before. I then created a psychological model to differentiate between *identity* and *roles*. It turned out to be the missing link in mastering professional selling.

Do You Know the Difference Between What You "R" and Who You "I"? Successful People Do!

Ever wonder why some people excel and others seem incapable of doing anything right? You probably know people who hit home runs no matter what they do. We call them "naturals." They're just plain good.

But how did they get that way? Surely you know more people who aren't naturals. They not only don't hit home runs every time, but they seldom hit home runs at all. What's different about these people?

More important, if you're not a natural, why not? What's different about you? And what can you do, if anything, to become a natural? Or to become a person who hits home runs most of the time?

Many years ago, I discovered a rule of human relationships that determines how well a person will perform in all areas of life, regardless of education, practice, and training. It's a very simple rule, and once you learn it, you can no doubt put it to use to improve the quality of your life. Before I explain it to you, however, I want you to complete the following exercise.

Imagine yourself on a deserted island. The sky is clear. The wind is calm. The sea is smooth. You will be on this island for only a few minutes. Imagine now that you arrived on this island without any roles. Roles such as husband, wife, CEO, accountant, sales manager, engineer, golfer, fisherman, and so on, do not exist on this island.

Now, using the scale that follows, rate yourself without any roles. Zero is the lowest end of the scale, and 10 is the highest end. Where do you rate yourself on that scale? What value do you place on yourself without any of the roles that you play out in life? Go ahead and mark the scale now.

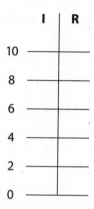

Next, take time to write a brief description of how you picture yourself without any roles.

_____

_____

_____

_____

_____

_____

OK, now you've returned from the island. How did you rate yourself? Once you stripped yourself of all your roles, you were left with your self-concept, your self-image, or your *identity*. If you rated yourself anything less than a perfect 10, you were wrong. You may believe you're something less than a 10, but believe me, your identity is worth *all* 10 points.

Chances are, you rated yourself less than a 10. Most people do. In my seminars, and those of my associates, we frequently hear these comments from audience members:

"Without my roles, I would be worthless."
"How could anyone be a 10—nobody is perfect."
"My roles make me what I am."
"You can't separate roles from whatever is left."
"I'm ready for the garbage pail if you take away my roles."

I think I can prove to you that your identity is worth a 10. I placed you on an island in the exercise because you are similar to an island. We are all like islands. We are surrounded by others, yet we live in our own worlds. Didn't you come into this world alone? Didn't you come into this world without any role? The answer is yes. Therefore, you can detach yourself from your roles, can't you? Of course you can. You've acquired these roles along the highways of life.

Your identity, since birth, has remained unchanged. Your roles never have and never will define your identity. You may think they do, but they don't. It's difficult to separate your identity from your role, but it's important to see that there's a difference.

From childhood, many of us were taught that our roles determined our worth in life. With the best of intentions, our parents told us that our success would be related to our position in life. Becoming educated was important. Getting a college degree would make or break us. Climbing the corporate ladder would make the difference. Jumping hurdle after hurdle would be important, and the higher the hurdle the better.

Like most of us, you probably were taught to believe that success is determined externally, not internally. Therefore, learning to feel good about yourself was a waste of time. In other words, what society thought of you was more important than what you thought of yourself.

Do you ever recall your parents asking questions like these:

> "Did you eat all your cereal?"
> "Are you playing nicely with your friends?"
> "How did you do on your exams?"
> "Did you make the basketball team?"
> "Did you get a good job?"

To answer those questions positively, you had to have accomplished something. The list of similar questions is endless, and parents ask them of their children day after day.

Meanwhile, how often did your parents say:

> "We love you because you are you."
> "It is OK to like yourself."
> "Don't measure yourself by what others accomplish."

Even our school system reinforces this emphasis on accomplishment, or role, as opposed to internal success. Did you ever get a report card that measured your *identity achievement?* Of course not. There was no room for this measurement. Imagine a report card that read: "Jim doesn't do well with numbers; he is having a little trouble with reading; his penmanship requires improvement... but, be happy, Mr. and Mrs. Smith, because your son has a healthy identity." Sadly, even today, most report cards end right before the "but."

None of this is to place blame on parents, teachers, or anyone, for that matter. I merely want to point out that while we were growing up, much time was devoted to making us believe that we were *worth more if we achieved something.* If we failed, we got the message that we were *worth less.* And the message didn't say we were worth less as role performers. It said we were *worth less.* Period. As human beings, we were worthless. So in time, we mistakenly accepted *role failure as identity failure.* We were never told there was a difference.

There *is* a difference! When you were born, wouldn't you rate your identity as a 10? Sure you would. How could you rate it anything less? As a human being, your value was of maximum worth. And it has never changed. Role success or failure is merely a measurement of how well you are doing in your acquired roles. But in no way do roles affect your value as a human being.

Can you accept that both *identity* and *role* are important factors in your life? Perhaps you're saying, "Yes, but so what?"

Well, let me tell you. It makes a lot of difference to your overall success. You can only be in one of three psychological positions. You're either a winner, a nonwinner, or an at-leaster. And you can decide which position is for you!

On the identity scale above, winners rank themselves somewhere between 7 and 10. Regardless of how well they're performing in their roles, winners feel pretty good about themselves. Their self-image is healthy. In fact, they see themselves as winners. They're the naturals.

The nonwinners, meanwhile, rate themselves between 0 and 3. They allow their role performances to affect how they feel about themselves. Unfortunately, the nonwinners consistently do poorly in most of their roles.

Lastly, the at-leasters rate themselves between 3 and 7 on the scale. They like themselves only when things are going well in their roles. During those times when they're experiencing role failure, they don't like themselves. At-leasters don't win, but they don't lose either.

What we know about winners, nonwinners, and at-leasters is that *they can perform in their roles only in a manner that is consistent with how they see themselves conceptually.* In other words: your role performance corresponds to your identity rating, every time.

Here's how that works. Meet Eddie, a salesperson. On the identity scale, Eddie values himself an I-5. He has spent years allowing his role performance to affect the way he feels about himself. This is a result of Eddie's lifelong training. He was taught to believe that his worth is a result of how well he performs in his roles.

Eddie's a textbook at-leaster. One day he turns in a stellar performance. He closes 10 out of 10 sales calls in a row. There's no doubt that on this day Eddie is an R-10 in his role as a salesperson. But then what happens?

That night, Eddie sits on the edge of his bed looking at his 10 closed sales. With his money in hand, he looks over his shoulder at his identity value—remember, it's only an I-5 in his mind—and he says to himself, "I'm good, but I ain't that good."

The next day, Eddie finds a way to adjust his role performance. Since he doesn't believe conceptually that he deserves to win, he subconsciously begins to do whatever he must to return to what I call his "comfort zone." An individual's comfort zone usually straddles the I rating. For example, Eddie rated himself an I-5; therefore, his comfort zone was R-4 to R-6.

Remember, Eddie can perform in his roles only in the manner that is consistent with how he sees himself conceptually. He feels comfortable only when he relates to the concept he holds of himself, an I-5. Therefore, Eddie races to his comfort zone every chance he can.

Look what happens on a day when Eddie experiences the low of lows. He goes 0 to 10 in sales. His I-5 rating tells him that he's better than that. "I'm not the greatest," he says that night, "but I ain't as bad as all that!" So he adjusts himself by doing whatever he has to do at a subconscious level to get back to his comfort zone, and for a while at least, his role performance improves.

Now, how can Eddie become a winner? What does he do? Traditional sales training says the answer is for Eddie to work on role performance. He's got to learn better selling techniques and strategies. He needs to go to seminars, read books, attend workshops, listen to CDs, and *get motivated!* Chances are, Eddie will tell us he's been doing that all his life, and things haven't changed all that much. In fact, things never will change much using the traditional methodologies. No matter how hard Eddie works at training the R side of his life, his performance will always remain average. He will remain an at-leaster as long as he sees himself as an I-5.

> Successful people recognize there's a difference between what you R and who you I.

Unfortunately, traditional sales training programs concentrate only on improving the R factor. As long as these programs ignore the I factor, they will fail to help people improve not just their selling skills but their lives overall. *Training that fails to address both the I and R factors will not result in permanent improvements.*

Perhaps now you understand why it makes no sense to use role performance as a measurement of your value as a human being. Success in the sales profession, for example, measures only how good you are as a salesperson. Failure as a salesperson, while unpleasant and painful, should not affect your value as a human being.

Successful people recognize there's a difference between what you R and who you I.

If you keep your R and I in perspective and you work on both factors, your quality of life improves overall. Here's a simple mind game that may help you.

Imagine yourself back on that island. This time there's a castle on the island, and the castle represents your I. Around the castle, there's a moat filled with crocodiles. A drawbridge leads across the moat to the real world, which is full of inhabitants. The real world represents your R.

When you awake each morning, and before you engage in your daily work, you are on the island, alone in your castle. No one can enter your castle because the drawbridge has been lifted high. You're an I-10 as you begin your day and venture across the drawbridge to the R world.

Once you've arrived in the R world, you begin to interact with the inhabitants. Some of your interactions are nonthreatening and rewarding. Other interactions, however, are full of conflict. Some result in role failure.

The longer you're in the R world, the more stressful you feel. Once the stress takes its toll, you must return to your I world. You've got to get back across the drawbridge, raise the bridge to keep out the inhabitants of the R world, and enter your castle. From there, you can look at the R world with a clear perspective.

Your island is your safety net. No one can enter your I without permission. No one can affect you or hurt you. You're in complete control. Your I remains a 10, where it ought to be!

SANDLER TRAINING TIP

The I/R Theory. We find that one good way for people to get their heads around David Sandler's revolutionary distinction between identity and role is for them to start thinking of selling as a game. If you're playing a game, with clear rules, you're usually safe. So, the rules of this game are that you reach out to people you don't know. It's not personal. How could someone you don't even know make a personal attack against you by (for instance) hanging up on you? This is a total stranger! When people who don't even know you decide to hang up on you, or when they say something you don't like, you can make that part of the game you are playing, part of the performance you are giving. Good salespeople are a whole lot like actors. They pretend to be dumb sometimes because that suits their purposes. They pretend to struggle with issues with which they actually aren't struggling. Sometimes they even pretend to be interested. They know it's a game. They know the people they call aren't hanging up on them as people. Prospects are hanging up on the role they took on, on the game they decided to play.   —DHM

The I/R Theory explains the importance of separating what you R, that is, the roles you play, from who you I, that is, your identity. It was my first stab at saying that a successful sales training program must combine *technique training* and *correct behavior* with an *understanding of human dynamics*. When you combine the three, and add other elements, the combination is called *reinforcement training*. It's the only way to succeed in sales without the emotional turmoil and humiliation that always accompany traditional selling.

People who understand human dynamics can separate what they R from who they I. If they are in sales, they can make cold calls all day, and then they can go home and never think about selling the rest of the evening. It's rare to find such people in sales because salespeople thrive on approval, and approval for the traditionally trained salesperson comes only from making the sales. Therefore, they do whatever they have to do to make the sales. They're willing to hear 100 noes to find one person who will say yes. They're willing to be manipulative just to get a check. And when they hear that one yes, it's like a drug. They'll do whatever is necessary to hear it again and again. It's a trap. They can't get out of it unless they believe that it's OK to accept a no, or to accept failure. The problem is that no one teaches salespeople how to accept failure.

It's Important to Learn to Fail!

Failure is universal. It's part of the human experience. It's important to learn how to fail because the only way to achieve anything is to risk failing.

Why is it so difficult to risk failing? I think it's because we don't understand failure, and we don't see that failure includes an upside. With all of our success programming and conditioning, it would be difficult to suddenly begin saying, "I just can't wait to fail again." However, it's normal to fail. It's healthy to fail. And the most successful and professional salespeople would never allow failure to stand in their path to success.

Like anything else, we can learn to fail. We can learn to accept failure so that risking failure doesn't have to be so difficult. Here are Sandler's Five Steps to Failure, a process that offers the upside to failing:

1. **Disbelief.** When you fail, your mind will automatically deny it. You can't believe it, or you simply don't want to. It's always a mistake to arrive at major decisions during the first stage of failure, but

unfortunately, that's what most people do. They fail at something, they step back, and they say, "I can't believe this has happened to me." Then, they go off and do something else. When you fail, understand that disbelief is the first hurdle to cross. Go ahead, just accept it! Shake your head and believe it happened.

2. **Fear.** When people fail, they get frightened. "I set out to accomplish this goal, I didn't do it, and now I can't believe this has happened to me. I'm scared." Unfortunately, fear is an emotion that immobilizes most people. They get scared, and they don't know what to do. That's why they frequently decide to do the wrong thing. Instead, welcome the fear. Anticipate it like an old friend. And let fear become the survival mechanism that gets you motivated all over again.

3. **Anger.** Once fear sets in, most people think their world is going to crumble. That's when they get angry. Sometimes they go off and do something really stupid, such as throw a golf club into a window, smash a fist through a wall, quit their job, or cause physical harm to themselves or someone they love. It doesn't have to be so bad. Accept the anger. Get mad! But then cool down.

4. **Acceptance.** Realize that all you did was fail. It's normal. Happens to everyone. It's not the end of the world. Accept responsibility for whatever happened, and get ready to move on.

5. **Despair.** Once people accept what happened, it's normal for them to feel depressed. When you begin to feel despair, that's good! The failure process has been completed. Try not to make major decisions even at this point of the process. Instead, in those quiet moments of despair, try to figure out the lessons that you can learn from your failure. Good things do come out of failure. When you fail, you can begin to understand yourself better. That leads you to become more objective. This is a good time to evaluate your priorities. And perhaps you'll come away from it all with a new attitude.

The best thing about failure is that it strengthens your "gut" system. At Sandler, we frequently say, "No guts, no gain." When you fail, you've got two choices to make. You can either go to the curb and suck your thumb, or you can get on with your life. Perhaps you can fail often enough, and quickly enough, that your gut system will actually look forward to failure.

The most successful people are people who have learned how to fail!

I didn't arrive at these conclusions overnight, or all by myself. I had some help during my apprentice years. After I purchased my distributorship, I followed my predecessor's practice of placing ads in the business opportunity section of the local newspaper to recruit sales representatives. It was a constant exercise of recruiting and training people, and the end result was easily predictable. They'd last a week or two, maybe a few months, and they'd be gone. Even my home office, which recruited distributors and salespeople, experienced almost 100 percent turnover in the business. Of course, the home office made money by collecting an up-front fee from the distributors and then selling the motivational packages. For a while, it was a money machine, but it was a pitiful merry-go-round to watch.

One afternoon, in response to my ad in the *Baltimore Sun*, a professor from the University of Maryland visited me. He said he had just moved from Connecticut, and he was looking for work to supplement his teaching salary. "I thought I could get into the business world," he told me, "but I don't know how. Can you help me?"

I explained that he didn't fit the profile of the person I needed, but during our conversation we discovered our common interest in transactional analysis. Coincidentally, he was a psychologist, well grounded in TA theories, so I offered him the opportunity to help me create a sales training program. "What I'm doing—calling on businesses—you don't want to do," I said. (Obviously, I was still struggling myself.) "But since you're a specialist in TA, I'll buy two hours a week of your time. You come to my office, and I'll ask you some questions, and let's see where it goes from there."

He accepted my offer, and we worked together for a year. I asked him questions like these:

"Why don't salespeople like to make phone calls?"
"What's behind my personal call reluctance?"

"How does self-image affect my ability to sell?"
"Do salespeople always have to sacrifice their self-esteem to
    make a sale?"
"What are some games that salespeople play?"
"What are some games that prospects play?"

The professor was a very creative and thoughtful teacher, and he
helped me enormously. The answers that I had been searching for
eventually crystallized during my sessions with him.

We recorded our conversations, hired someone to transcribe the
tapes, and then edited the materials. The end result was a package of
12 audiotapes and a workbook that I titled *Dynamics of Self-Awareness*.
I introduced the package through my distributorship. It was a self-
therapy course, especially for salespeople, and it immediately helped
them improve their performance. *Dynamics of Self-Awareness* was
right in step with the times—many corporations were taking their
people to seminars to teach them about self-awareness—and salespeople loved it. But the program wasn't just for salespeople. Any
healthy, coping person could listen to the audiotapes, complete the
exercises in the workbook, and come away feeling better, regardless of
his or her profession.

By this time, in 1972, I knew I was onto something revolutionary.
The techniques worked for me, and I no longer hated selling. I no longer woke up feeling sick because I had to prospect for sales that day.
I didn't perspire when I picked up the telephone to call a stranger. I
loved my work, and my bank account reflected my accomplishments.
I progressed from annual earnings of $50,000 to the mid-six figures
within a few years. For some reason, however, I still had the feeling
that I was missing something.

Are You Like the Spider?

Ever hear the story of the turtle and the spider?

The turtle is resting at the side of a creek, and a spider is next to
him. The spider says to the turtle, "Do you think you are going to cross
that creek anytime soon?"

The turtle says, "Yep, I'll probably swim across that creek."

So the spider says, "Can I go with you? I can't swim."

The turtle looks at the spider and says, "Are you insane? If I put you on my back and start swimming across the creek, you're going to bite me, and when you do, I'm going to die."

The spider responds, "That's ridiculous. Think about it. We're halfway across the creek. I'm on your back, I bite you. You're going down. Where am I going?"

The turtle thinks about that and says, "You're going down with me." He pauses for a moment and continues, "OK, hop on."

The turtle swims about half the distance across the creek with the spider on his back, and then it happens. Zap! The spider bites the turtle's neck, and they're both drowning.

The turtle looks up at the spider and says, "Why?"

And the spider says, "It's my nature."

People are a lot like the spider. We do what's natural for us. If we rate ourselves as I-5s, then we are. Even on days when we're R-10s, our nature will force us to return to mediocrity. People adjust to whatever they think is natural for them. It's their nature.

SANDLER TRAINING TIP

Ninety percent of success resides between the ears. David Sandler's legacy is not so much a legacy of technique—although the techniques he taught us were masterful. And his legacy is not really a legacy of behavior—although the daily accountabilities he identified can lead to extraordinary success. I believe the most important legacy he left for salespeople—and for everyone else—has to do with transforming our attitudes, transforming what we believe to be our natural state of mind. His legacy is helping people make mediocrity a thing of the past via the principle that 90 percent of success resides between the ears.   —DHM

The first year that I owned my distributorship, Edna and I attended a national convention at the Greenbriar Hotel in West Virginia. Distributors from around the country attended the meeting, and I was eager to meet as many of them as I could. These were the giants of my new industry. For months, I had listened to many of them on audiotapes, and I thought they held all the answers. One night during the convention, the home office sponsored an awards banquet, and 50 distributors won trophies for their sales accomplishments. I didn't win a thing. I turned to Edna and said, "This will never happen again. I'm not coming to these conventions to watch other people get awards. I must be doing something wrong."

So during the next few years, whenever I could get away from selling, Edna and I traveled the country to visit these magical people. One by one I was disappointed by what I discovered. They were all struggling. I went from Dallas to Denver, from Washington to Virginia, and interviewed every distributor who agreed to spend time with me. Most of them were starving. There was nothing consistent about their lives. A year of success was easily followed by a year of failure, but they faked their way through it, just as they had been taught to do. These were the stars of the distributor network, and most of them were miserable.

Something was obviously wrong, but I continued as a distributor until 1974. During that time, except for that first convention, I never had a year in which I didn't win an award. I set numerous sales records, too, using the techniques that I was discovering on my own.

In spite of the success that I experienced with the principles that the professor and I revealed in *Dynamics of Self-Awareness*, the program wasn't everything it needed to be. In fact, it didn't work for most people. At first blush, everyone who bought the program thought it was the greatest information he or she had ever heard. I'd sell it for $600, but that was the end of it. The clients who listened to the program agreed with it, but they did nothing. How could that be? I sold a program that unlocked the secrets to success in sales, and people would not use it, even though they thought it was right!

Finally, out of desperation, I said to several of my clients, "Look, why don't you come to the Holiday Inn every other Thursday evening where I'm going to teach a class based on *Dynamics of Self-Awareness*. Come and join some of my other clients." And the next thing I knew, I had 250 people in a hotel room on Thursday nights. One night, I taught from my motivational package, using the traditional sales techniques (at that time, I still didn't know any better). Another night, I taught the I/R Theory and other elements related to human dynamics in sales. And suddenly, people started to use the material! They returned to the hotel every other Thursday night to share their successes and their failures, and to hear my next lesson.

Those Thursday nights proved to be the third element of my professional sales training program. It seems so simple now. Those Thursday night meetings became "therapy sessions" for my clients. Not therapy in the real sense, as you'd expect to get from a trained psychologist, but a coaching session. If there was a point between doing nothing to improve your sales performance and going to therapy, it was Thursday nights! And I created it only out of my desperate desire to get my clients to use my materials.

SANDLER TRAINING TIP

Finding power in reinforcement. In the field of professional sports, when you hit the top of your game, do you practice more or practice less? More, of course. For real superstars, the commitment, the focus, and the team orientation only increase at that point. It's the same with the very best salespeople and the very best leaders. You've got to practice. You've got to rehearse. You've got to lock in new distinctions. Since David Sandler founded our company over four decades ago, our organizational mantra has always been "Reinforcement, reinforcement, reinforcement." It's still our mantra. We know that incremental learning, coupled with ongoing reinforcement training, is the only process that delivers sustainable change. Period.

Of course, people *want* instantaneous impact change. They want to see positive, enduring changes immediately. But our experience is that that kind of change is going to be sustainable over time only if you create a solid ongoing reinforcement program to back up the learning. Ideally, that reinforcement takes place in a social setting, in real time, with peers you respect. Mobile devices and online relationships are fine as supplements, but the most effective reinforcement happens in this in-person environment. David Sandler was the true pioneer in our industry when it came to incrementally growing successful professional salespeople and sales leaders through continuous reinforcement. We owe our dominant position in today's marketplace, at least in part, to his emphasis on this point.   —DHM

Coaching was the secret weapon of reinforcement training. It was OK to listen to audiotapes. But there are only certain times of the day when the audiotapes will help you. If you're feeling good about yourself, it's easy to respond positively to the audiotapes. But what happens when you just missed a sale? Are you mentally receptive to learning from audiotapes? No! It's easier to analyze what you did wrong and fix it shortly after doing it than waiting for your negative mindset to improve so that you can respond positively. And that's why salespeople need a coach. On Thursday nights, I became a coach for my clients, and they became coaches for one another, and for me.

Meanwhile, my business was booming! My own sales staff, the people who used to come and go like people through a revolving door, attended the Thursday night meetings, and immediately their sales performances improved. Now, instead of the occasional sale, they sold programs every day, and they recruited more students for Thursday's class. Some of them started sponsoring classes of their own. And with every class, the combination of tapes and coaching and sharing with one another—what we now call "reinforcement training"—made it possible for people from all types of professions to succeed in sales.

> I became a coach for my clients, and they became coaches for one another, and for me.

You can succeed in sales, too, and in the following chapters I'll show you how by demonstrating the various steps of the Sandler reinforcement training program.

4

CONDITIONING YOURSELF FOR SUCCESS IN SALES

To get to the top of the sales profession,

you've got to practice, practice, practice.

Find a system that works, and learn it.

Spend enough time getting to know

it, and soon you will own it. And then,

even under pressure, you will deliver.

—DAVID H. SANDLER

Becoming a good professional salesperson requires the same type of training that other good professionals endure. Athletes, physicians, college professors, firefighters—you name the profession, and the people at the top pay a price *every day* to stay there. The price they pay is their *conditioning.* That's not the same as the system they follow to succeed in their profession, but conditioning is an important part of the total success equation. Conditioning is the "hardware" as opposed to the "software." Conditioning is a way of life. It's a set of rules, sometimes philosophical, but always practical. Follow the rules and you'll always be conditioned to make the best use of the system.

Through the years, Sandler Training has charted the success and failure of thousands of sales professionals. We've documented that those who become top sales performers, and those who remain at the top year after year, condition themselves daily for success. They adhere to the following 10 basic conditioning rules that are important for every salesperson.

1. Stay on the right side of the Trouble Line. Salespeople have a choice to make every day. They can either be on Pay Time or No-Pay Time. Trouble occurs, however, when they spend too much time on the No-Pay Time side of the line.

Pay Time is from 9 a.m. to 5 p.m., or whichever part of the day or night is best for presenting your product or service to prospects. This is that special time when prospects are inclined to see you, when you call on referrals, set appointments, and service your customers.

No-Pay Time is important, too, but it's set aside for planning, conditioning, learning more about your product or service, and attending meetings. No-Pay Time usually occurs after 5 p.m. and before 9 p.m.

Many salespeople confuse Pay Time and No-Pay Time, but top salespeople always know the difference between the two. They recognize that too much time spent on the left side of the line will almost always result in poorer sales performance. The goal of the top performers is to stay on the right side of the Trouble Line.

When you perform No-Pay Time activities during Pay Time hours, you create a worse problem than simply hurting your sales performance. If you're supposed to be doing one thing, and you know it, but you do something else, two negatives occur:

> Even if your employer won't pay you commissions instead of salary, mentally put yourself on commission. When you do, it will be easier to keep yourself on the right side of the Trouble Line.

- You feel guilty because you're violating your conditioning.
- You're less productive because you're doing the wrong thing.

Do you see how that leads to trouble?

If you're sitting in your office during Pay Time, but you're spending hours planning, reading trade literature, conducting meetings, and moving prospect cards from the left side of the desk to the right side, or even if you're in your car driving from the west side of town to the east side, you may say you're working, but you know you're working on the wrong side of the Trouble Line.

It's easier for salaried salespeople to violate this conditioning rule than it is for those who get paid on commission. The salaried salespeople may not feel the urgency that comes with a commission-only job. They're going to collect the same dollar amount week after week, so time management is a less critical issue for salaried employees. However, if you are salaried and you're spending too much time on the wrong side of the Trouble Line, you may be just a heartbeat away from termination.

Salary is just another form of commission to a top-performing salesperson. In fact, there's no such thing as salary in the sales profession. If you now take a salary, I suggest you stop it. Get yourself on commission. Even if your employer won't pay you commissions instead of salary, mentally put yourself on commission. When you do, it will be easier to keep yourself on the right side of the Trouble Line.

Another trick to help you use Pay Time productively is to set goals. I'm not talking about annual goals and five-year plans. They have their place, but I'm talking about setting daily goals. Top sales performers condition themselves by beginning every day with goals. "Today, I want to accomplish the following," and they either record their goals on paper, or they note them mentally. I suggest you keep a daily journal (see rule 8) to help you maintain quality time management.

It's easy to recognize salespeople who violate the Trouble Line Rule. They're the hysterical-acting people. Instead of pacing themselves, they fall behind in their work. At the end of the month they scramble to make their quotas, or suddenly they've scheduled back-to-back sales calls three days in a row. This hysterical activity is nonproductive. It results in panic. And it occurs because the salesperson failed to consistently spend time on the right side of the Trouble Line.

If you want to get to the top of your sales profession, be consistent. Stay on the right side of the Trouble Line, and make your Pay Time productive.

2. Burn your bridges. If you want to become a top performer in the sales profession, commit yourself to it full time. The Monday morning that I quit my $12,500-a-year job in the snack business was a turning point in my life.

> When you choose sales as your profession, commit wholeheartedly to yourself, your family, your product or service, and your prospects.

It was difficult to make the break, but it would have been impossible to climb to the top of the selling profession had I not done it.

When you choose sales as your profession, commit wholeheartedly to yourself, your family, your product or service, and your prospects. You know that it won't be easy to succeed in sales. You don't expect prospects to roll over and say yes every time you make a presentation.

But once you make the decision to get into the profession, burn your bridges and force yourself to succeed. *Live to sell, but don't sell to live.* If you begin with the attitude that "if this doesn't work, I can always go back to my old profession," you've already lost the battle.

Top sales performers don't get to second base with one foot on first!

Don't Practice in Front of the Prospect

Earlier I explained that I was an avid golfer, and one of the activities that I especially enjoyed was the Monday pro-am tournament. Every Monday, the pro at our country club invited three other golfers to join him in a tournament at another country club. Pros and amateurs teamed up and played against each other, and I loved it.

I was so dedicated and determined to play well that if we had a 9 a.m. tee time, I would show up at 7 with a bag of a hundred practice golf balls. I'd go over to the practice range and use every iron in my bag to get ready for the tournament.

One morning just before tee time, Cos, the pro from my club, came out to the practice range. I was soaking in perspiration trying to get my game in shape, and I saw Cos drop three balls on the ground. He hit a nine iron, then a five iron, and a three wood. And then he started walking away.

I said, "Cos, this is an important tournament. You've gotta practice, get ready, warm up." Cos turned to me and said, "Sandler, if you didn't bring it with you, you're not going to find it here."

What a great practice story! The time to practice is not in front of the prospect!

3. Get mentally and emotionally tough. Professional selling can be cruel. Prospects are frequently better conditioned than the salespeople who call on them, and consequently they can destroy a salesperson in a phone call or during a chance meeting. On a day-to-day basis, even a

> Four things can happen to you in a selling situation. You can get a "yes," a "no," a "no" with a lesson, or an "I want to think it over."

good salesperson hears "no" more often than any other word. Can you think of a worse profession for people who thrive on acceptance?

The word "no" comes with the territory in sales. So does failure. Unfortunately, traditional sales trainers never say it's OK to fail, or that you should stop when you hear the word "no." But top sales performers know better. They learn from their failures. And if they can't hear a "yes," they'd rather get a "no." They want to avoid anything in between. And that requires them to remain tough mentally and emotionally.

Four things can happen to you in a selling situation. You can get a "yes," a "no," a "no" with a lesson, or an "I want to think it over."

A "yes" always feels great. It pumps you up and motivates you to find another prospect.

A "no" doesn't feel great, but at least you know where you stand.

A "no" with a lesson isn't so bad. You know where you stand, and when you get off the phone, or back to your car, you may be able to turn a negative into something learned.

You want to avoid the "I want to think it over" answer because there's nothing worse in sales. What does it mean? When you go back to your car and begin to critique yourself, what do you say? "What happened in that sales call? Where do I stand? Could I have closed the sale with a little more perseverance? Should I have done this, or that?"

The sad thing is that most salespeople are satisfied to hear an "I want to think it over." It gives them a false sense of security. After all, will a sales manager fire a guy who says he's got 84 proposals on the street? He will eventually if those proposals don't materialize into sales.

> The sad thing is that most salespeople are satisfied to hear an "I want to think it over."

Always go for a "yes" or a "no."

4. Maintain a healthy self-esteem. If you're going to be a top sales performer, you've got to feel good about yourself. When you feel good about who you are and what you can do, you can work more effectively.

Everyone wants to feel good psychologically, but some people can feel good only at the expense of other people. People with poor self-images can't feel good about themselves, so they'll frequently attack anyone who exhibits a better self-image. Consequently, salespeople make easy targets.

Here's a familiar story. The salesperson goes out to call on a prospect. He parks his car, straightens his tie, puts on his suit coat, and walks up three flights of stairs to the prospect's office. When he gets there, he's stopped by a pane of glass with a hole in it. Behind the glass is an older woman, earning a minimum wage to answer the phone, open the mail, and "greet" visitors. Our salesperson looks wonderful; our receptionist looks frazzled.

The salesperson takes his embossed business card and a $250 Cross pen from his $500 Gucci briefcase and announces himself to the receptionist by saying, "Good morning, I'd like to see the chief executive."

Never looking up, the receptionist responds, "You got an appointment?"

In that instant, our salesperson is wiped out. He's done. Of course he doesn't have an appointment. But now he's also been stripped of his self-esteem.

Why would a receptionist, or anyone, act that way? On an intellectual level, she doesn't mean to offend a visitor. She's doing her job, and it's a tough one. Most of the time, she doesn't feel good about what she's doing. She's got problems at home, she doesn't earn enough money, and her boss is harassing her. The only way she can feel OK, some of the time, is to steal self-esteem from someone else. One of the ways the receptionist gets to feel good about herself is to see someone like our salesperson walk in looking terrific, and crawl out looking stressed. When he leaves, she can say to herself, "Hey, things may not be OK for me, but compared to that salesperson, I'm OK!"

So what's a salesperson to do? Don't take interaction personally. If you do, you'll end up feeling Not-OK about yourself. If you make the common mistake of accepting rejection in your self-esteem, you're finished for the day. You'll immediately run to the No-Pay Time side of the Trouble Line.

Protect yourself. Develop a healthy self-image. (Now's a good time to review the I/R Theory in Chapter 3.) It's not important what people say, do, or think about you. What's important is how you feel about yourself.

5. Cultivate a support group. We live in an I-centered world. When you call on prospects, they're not concerned about you. They're concerned about themselves. And you're the same way, aren't you? We're all concerned about what's most important to us.

Since professional salespeople are constantly calling on other people who are I centered, it's important for the professional salesperson to find a support group. If you want to be a top performer, find other top performers, or others who are on their way to the top, and spend time with them. Just be careful that you don't spend this time on the wrong side of the Trouble Line!

The coaching session that I offered to my clients when I couldn't get them to use my products created a supportive environment for them. We all learned to sell better by helping one another. That's why Sandler sponsors weekly President's Clubs in cities across the United States and around the world. These types of activities are critical in the conditioning of top sales performers. They provide the reinforcement training that's necessary to succeed.

6. Know when to use the product knowledge. For whatever reason—I suppose it's due to their traditional training—salespeople think they've always got to tell what they know. Instead, they should practice silence.

Many salespeople think they can impress prospects by spilling everything they know about their product or service. Somehow, that seems to give them more confidence to sell. It's

> Practice silence.

important for you to know as much as possible about your product or service, but the same is not always true for your prospect. Or at least it's not true during the initial sales call.

Here's an example. A couple enters a furniture store and finds a salesperson. He's proud of everything in the store, and he's happy to show the couple a beautiful chest. The wife comments that the piece would be perfect in her dining room, and the husband is showing buying signs as well. The salesperson begins mentally counting his commission. He's so excited! He says, "Let me tell you one more thing about this beautiful chest. All the drawers are on ball bearings." He then slides a drawer in and out to show the couple the ease with which it rolls from the chest. Suddenly, there's a strange look on the wife's face. She looks at her husband and says, "I swallowed a ball bearing when I was two and nearly choked to death." She's no longer interested. The salesperson says, "I'll show you something else," but the couple is gone. So much for product knowledge.

A good rule of thumb, which we will cover in depth a little later in this book, is this: sell today and educate tomorrow!

SANDLER SELLING TIP

Sell today and educate tomorrow. In recent years, this principle has taken on particular importance for those tasked with selling solutions that involve information and communication technology. These tools change so often, and so disruptively, that we give up a huge marketplace advantage to our competitors whenever we attempt to deliver features-and-benefits "lectures" to our prospects. Features and benefits don't tell you about the buyer's pain. The fact that the people in development (or marketing, for that matter) work from spec sheets, or even write brochures about the products, does not mean that spec sheets form the best agenda for a discussion with a prospect.   —DHM

---

7. **Know your competition.** Most salespeople are so concerned about product knowledge and looking good in front of a prospect that they forget about their competition. Top sales performers, on the other hand, spend time going to the competition's seminars, reading their brochures, and learning their strengths and weaknesses.

One day I made a cold call on a Trane Air Conditioning franchisee in Baltimore. During the interview I found out that he had just spent a lot of money with a famous sales trainer, and he liked his program. He said to me, "I just spent several thousand dollars for this program, and while you may have some good materials, I can't spend any money with you."

Knowing that I was selling reinforcement training and that he had purchased traditional sales training, I said, "Well, how are you enjoying the reinforcement part of the program?"

He looked at me and said, "What reinforcement?"

"You look like a smart guy," I said, "and I can't imagine that you would have spent money on training without getting backup support to make sure it works."

He said the support wasn't offered, and he didn't think to ask about it.

I continued: "Are you willing to spend $500 to make sure your program works? I'll come to your office once a week and show your staff the power of reinforcement training using the material you bought. I just want you to agree that if after using your material I think my material is more effective, you will give your people the option to use my material."

He agreed. And a month later, I had a new client! At the time, there were 75 Trane franchisees in the United States. The Baltimore franchisee just so happened to head up Trane's training committee, and one day he invited me to make a presentation to Trane's board of directors. I ended up running training programs for franchisees across the country, and for Trane's home office in Wisconsin. That initial $500 fee led to hundreds of thousands of dollars I earned from Trane throughout the years, and it happened because I knew the difference between my product and the competition's.

As I developed my own selling system, knowledge of my competition became an important component.

8. Keep a journal. Unfortunately, most salespeople set goals like New Year 's resolutions. On January 1, they make a 365-day commitment. By January 2, they have forgotten what they had committed to do.

Top sales performers set daily goals. They realize that they have two choices in this profession. They can either become part of their own plan, or they can become part of someone else's plan. Goal setting helps them take control of every day.

I started keeping a daily journal as an apprentice salesman. I recommend it for everyone today. I call it the Attitude/Behavior (A/B) Journal (see example that follows), and here's how it works:

Date _____

ATTITUDE/BEHAVIOR JOURNAL

MY "I" GOAL FOR TODAY IS:

_____
_____
_____
_____
_____
_____
_____

HISTORICAL REVIEW (END OF DAY):

_____
_____
_____
_____
_____
_____
_____

MY "R" GOAL FOR TODAY IS:

_____
_____
_____
_____
_____
_____
_____

HISTORICAL REVIEW (END OF DAY):

_____
_____
_____
_____
_____
_____
_____

FACE-TO-FACES   _____
FUTURES   _____
CLOSED FILES   _____
REFERRALS   _____
OTHER: _____
_____   _____
_____   _____
SOLD   _____

ATTITUDE ASSESSMENT

I (0–10)   _____
WHY: _____
_____
_____
R (0–10)   _____
WHY: _____
_____
_____

On the left side of the journal, record your I (identity) goal for the day. Select one goal that will help you strengthen your self-esteem. (You may want to review the I/R Theory in Chapter 3.)

Also on the left side of the page, note your R (role) goal for the day. For example, how many cold calls will you make today? Or, how many prospects will you see?

At the end of the day, write a review for each goal. Describe how well you met your goals for the day.

In the lower left corner of the A/B Journal, there's a list of topics that you will review on a daily basis. Not all of these topics will relate to your selling cycle, but it's important to review your progress daily.

"Face-to-faces," for example, refers to the number of times you're in front of a prospect, eyeball to eyeball, using your selling system. You keep track of the face-to-faces because many of them turn into futures. A "future" is someone who hasn't said "no" but is qualified to say "yes." Some futures will turn into sales. If you have 5, 10, or 20 futures in your A/B Journal, there's a good chance you'll make a sale farther down the road.

SANDLER SELLING TIP

Face-to-face. In the digital age, a Skype or similar videoconference meeting with a prospect who isn't in the same room with you but can see you and be seen by you counts as a "face-to-face" meeting. This means your target market can be global!   —DHM

When I first realized the difference between identity and role, I started keeping my journal, and the real power of the journal was in reviewing it. I had made a call on the Sun Life Insurance Company, and on this particular day, I had made 12 to 13 cold calls and ended up with no sales. However, I got a future at Sun Life that day. So in my journal I noted that I was an I-10 and an R-2 because I had nothing to show for all those cold calls except one future.

Two weeks later I called on Sun Life, and the future turned into a $30,000 order. On that day, I noted in my journal that I was an I-10 and an R-10. Later, while doing a historical review of my progress, I realized that on the day I had thought I had accomplished nothing and I was an R-2, I had in fact made a sale. I just didn't collect it for two weeks. The review made me realize that if you do the work and practice the correct behaviors, you are always an I-10 and an R-10. If you do the work, it will eventually turn into money!

Someone recently asked me, "Who was your mentor?" and I said, "Pain." But when I talk about selling today and I think about the rewards I've reaped from this profession, I sometimes shake my head and say, "It was so simple. It was so easy!" And yet, I know that's not true. It seems like it was a cakewalk today, but it was painful at the time. Forcing myself to do the day-to-day mechanics required to succeed in the selling profession wasn't simple. Changing my behavior to get the end results that I needed wasn't easy. However, because I did what had to be done, I succeeded way beyond anyone's expectations. The rewards have been so plentiful, and enjoyable, that it's almost impossible to remember the pain today. Much of the credit for forcing myself to do the day-to-day mechanics that led to success belongs to the use of the A/B Journal.

9. You must work a prospecting system. If you've been in sales for more than six months and you're still making cold calls, you're on the wrong track. You're not going to reach the top. Traditional trainers might be proud of you for making these cold calls. But the top sales performers would tell you you're wasting time. There's a better way to get to the top.

You know about the 80/20 Rule, don't you? In sales, you get 80 percent of your business from 20 percent of your customers. Well, the same rule applies to prospecting. Go to your library and read the "Law of Compensation" in *Emerson's Essays*. In one simple sentence, it says: "Give more, get more." If you spend your time every day looking for someone who will consider your product or service, you're working harder, but not smarter.

Top sales performers spend 80 percent of their time servicing their clients and customers, and only 20 percent of their time prospecting. You can do that comfortably only when you understand Emerson's Law of Compensation. I learned about Emerson's Law of Compensation while listening to a recording from an insurance salesperson named Gandolfo. The recording was part of the collection that I sold at the time. Gandolfo explained that he was doing a mediocre job spending 80 percent of his time selling and 20 percent servicing his clients. Then he discovered the Law of Compensation. Gandolfo wondered what would happen if he reversed his work habits. What if he spent 80 percent of his time servicing his clients, and only 20 percent of his time selling? Once he made the switch and committed his time to his clients, he discovered that his clients started selling for him!

> Top sales performers spend 80 percent of their time servicing their clients and customers, and only 20 percent of their time prospecting.

And that's what happened when I stopped spending most of my time selling my product and started spending most of my time servicing people by teaching them reinforcement training. I was not satisfied by simply selling motivational programs. I wanted people to use the materials and benefit from them. But people told me that I was foolish for giving away my time. I disagreed. I believed in Emerson. I believed that by giving more, I would get more, and it happened. As much as 80 percent of my business was a result of referrals from people who benefited from my training and coaching.

Top sales performers get their clients and customers to prospect for them.

10. You must use a system for selling. In Chapter 1, I told you that if you don't use a system for selling, you will fall prey to your prospect's system *every time.* The prospect always uses a system, and it's never beneficial to the salesperson. To win the selling dance, and to reach the top of the selling profession, you must use a system.

While I'm going to tell you about my own selling system in Chapter 5, it's important for you to hear me say that it doesn't matter which system you use as long as it will get you to the top. However, any system that doesn't include both an emphasis on self-esteem (correct behavior or proper behavior) and an emphasis on technique training will not work.

As you know by now, I learned to sell the traditional way, and I had to invent my own selling system because traditional training was outdated. The prospects knew all the techniques and just what to say. One of the first techniques I learned to use was good only on Friday afternoons. When it was Friday afternoon and you were meeting with a prospect, and you wanted to close the sale, you would say, "The price goes up on Monday."

Wow! I couldn't wait for my first Friday afternoon after learning that close. I thought it was terrific, and that week I scheduled as many Friday afternoon appointments as I could fit into my schedule. Finally, Friday afternoon arrived, and I was with my first prospect. I made my presentation, and then I said, "Sir, you don't have to buy today, but the price goes up on Monday." And without missing a beat, he said, "That's the 'impending event close.' " He smiled. I cringed. He actually knew the name of the technique! He knew more than I did! It killed the rest of my day.

Many years ago, Ben Hogan was competing in the U.S. Open. He was one shot out of the lead, and he needed to make a birdie on the eighteenth hole to win. Being 210 yards back from the green is a tough shot even for a professional, but that's where Hogan found himself. With 5,000 people lining the course and waiting for his next stroke, Hogan had to hit the ball and get it close enough to the pin so that he could make a birdie and win the tournament. Could he do it? He was the best golfer in the world. But this was almost impossible.

Hogan went to his golf bag, selected his famous one iron, and lined up over the ball. With the crowd hushed, he hit the ball and set it down inches from the pin. One stroke later he knocked in the putt and won the tournament. To everyone who watched, it seemed unbelievable. The reporters ran up to Hogan, and one of them asked, "How did you do that under all the pressure?"

Calmly, Hogan responded. "I've hit that one iron 15,000 times in practice. All I had to do was hit it once more here and trust that all the practice would pay off."

The same is true in selling. To get to the top, you've got to practice, practice, practice. Find a system that works, and learn it. Remember, you can't teach a kid to ride a bike at a seminar. You'll need reinforcement training. Spend enough time getting to *know* the system, and soon you will *own* it. And then, even under pressure, you will deliver every time.

Master these 10 conditioning rules. If you do, you'll make it to the top of our profession.

5

BREAK THE RULES AND CLOSE MORE SALES

Traditional selling always left me feeling that I was underpaid, overworked, and worn out. I had to work too hard to get a sale, and once I got it, neither the thrill of the sale nor the money I could put in my pocket made me think it was worthwhile.

—DAVID H. SANDLER

If you want to maximize your earnings in sales and feel good about calling yourself a salesperson, you'll need to control every sales call. Traditional selling won't allow you to do that.

Sure, traditional salespeople usually can direct the flow of the conversation during a sales discussion, and they sometimes can lead their prospects to arrive at certain favorable conclusions, that is, a yes as opposed to a no. But they can't control the sales call every time. They can't lead a prospect to say "yes" without exhausting themselves and the prospect, and in the process they frequently forfeit their self-respect. Worst of all, they're the last to know when the sale is closed!

SANDLER SELLING TIP

You don't learn how to win by getting a "yes." You learn to win by getting a "no." If you fear and avoid the word "no" from prospects and customers, consider changing your focus. Don't fear the "no." Search for it!

Of course, getting a "yes" answer from a prospect does give you more confidence and self-assurance, and it certainly feels great. When a prospect says, "Yes, I will buy from you," that response takes you to the bank! We all like that. But as salespeople, we will get a lot more "no" answers than we will get "yes" answers. If the inevitability of those "no" responses demotivates us, we need to start looking at the "no" a little differently.

I have seen countless salespeople who were facing serious income challenges turn on a dime and begin generating all the revenue they targeted for themselves, and then some, just by changing their mental job description. They started to go into the field *looking* for a "no" answer, rather than a "yes" answer. And that one simple change transformed their careers!   —DHM

The prospect always holds the trump card, and the salesperson never knows if or when it's going to drop.

If you were to examine every sales course that's on the market today (excluding the Sandler Selling System), you would discover that each course is a variation of what we've known about selling for the past 25 to 50 years or more. Each course offers something different, but it's merely a rehash of archaic selling principles. Almost every course will concentrate on the proverbial dog-and-pony show, a presentation with lots of flare. There will be numerous creative ideas, some of them contradictory, to handle stalls and objections. Ultimately, the course will show you how to close the sale. Depending on who created the course and who's teaching it, some of these courses are more effective than others. No one course is bad, really. They're all just old.

The result of every one of these courses is that sometimes you do get a sale! But it's always a lot of work. The process itself creates so much tension and worry that you hardly ever enjoy making the sale. It's a process in which you try to trick the prospect into saying "yes." At the end of the day, whether you've made a sale or not, you're drained emotionally. And frequently you don't feel good about yourself, the process, or your profession. Consequently, sooner or later you're going to give up or get fired. Or if you're not that fortunate, you'll continue trying to do what can't be done.

Who could feel good about selling this way? Not me! Traditional selling always left me feeling that I was underpaid, overworked, and worn out. I had to work too hard to get a sale, and once I got it, neither the thrill of the sale nor the money I could put in my pocket made me think it was worthwhile. Therefore, I was never very motivated to begin the process all over again. Like most traditional salespeople, I was beaten before I got out the door most mornings.

And on those mornings when I was fired up and ready to take on the world, determined to get sale after sale that day, I had to face the rest of the downside of traditional selling. Everyone knows the techniques! Age-old traditional selling techniques have been used so often that only the neophyte prospect doesn't see them coming. As a result, it's easy for the prospect to take control of the sales call. The prospect drives the selling process and forces the salesperson to react. Ultimately, whether a sale occurs or not is up to the prospect. And the prospect is always the first to know the outcome!

There's a better way, I continued saying to myself time and time again in the early years of my sales career. One morning, prior to developing my own system, I sat in my car looking at a prospect's office door, and I said to myself, "I'm tired of doing the dog-and-pony show. I'm tired of being enthusiastic and giving million-dollar presentations to people who can't buy a cup of coffee, or say yes or no. The more I thought about it that morning, the angrier I got. "If I break the rules," I thought to myself, "I'll bet I make more sales."

In the car that morning, I described the ideal selling system. Here's how it would work:

> Prospects would deliver the presentations themselves.
> They would raise the stalls and objections, and they would resolve them.
> They would qualify themselves financially.
> They would close the sale.
> And finally, they would thank me for calling on them!

Now I could get used to that kind of selling! The pressure would be gone, I'd feel good about myself, my earnings would go up, up, up, and my customers would love me. Under that scenario, I'd live to sell, not sell to live. And so would you!

"Sounds good, but it's impossible," you say? Through the years, by trial and error, I created that ideal selling system. And as you continue reading this book, you'll discover how to make the system work for you.

The Sandler Selling System is a compilation of new and exciting ideas. It's not a reiteration of what you've already learned about selling. However, that means if you're to learn it, you must change what you're now doing in sales. Change never comes easily, but I assure you that if you adopt the changes required by the system, there are two huge payoffs awaiting you.

First, the intangible payoff: you'll become a more proficient, professional salesperson.

Second, the tangible payoff: you'll go to the bank more often. You'll put more money in your pocket.

Now, if neither payoff is important to you, stop reading! I can't help you. This book is of no value to you.

Something tells me you're still reading. You may not yet believe that the Sandler Selling System can deliver everything I've promised, but those two payoffs are important enough to you to maintain your interest. In fact, either one of the payoffs will be sufficient to far exceed the time you invest in reading the balance of this book.

So what is the Sandler Selling System?

Look at the submarine in Figure 5.1. Remember the World War II movies in which a depth charge hits dangerously close to the stern of the submarine?

The hero rushes belowdecks, summons the men out of the damaged compartment, slams the thick metal door, and spins the wheel as the compartment fills with water. There's no way to get back into that compartment, but the ship stays afloat. Tensions mount, the film rolls on, and the next compartment begins to fill with water. Again the hero moves the men forward, slams the thick metal door, spins the wheel, and the compartment fills with water. And so the process continues until each compartment fills with water, and the men continue moving forward to safety and to success.

The submarine story is an analogy of the Sandler Selling System. Each compartment of the submarine represents a step in the selling process. As you use the system, you advance your prospect—step-by-step—toward a successful sale. You finish the work in one compartment, and you close it. The prospect can't return to it.

The problem with traditional selling systems is that the prospect can run from one end of the submarine to the other, in and out of compartments, and the salesperson is forced to chase the prospect. That's why you're worn out at the end of a sales discussion! With the Sandler Selling System, you always remain in control. As you close each compartment, you move closer to the sale. And best of all, only *you* know

Figure 5.1 *The Sandler Submarine*

SM

Bonding & Rapport

Up-Front Contract

Pain

Budget

Decision

Fulfillment

Post-Sell

Sandler Training

that! You'll know that the sale has been closed even before you deliver the presentation. Sometimes, you don't even have to deliver the presentation!

Could anything be easier, or more exciting?

Let's look at the compartments of the Sandler Submarine.

The Bonding and Rapport step of the Sandler Selling System shows you how to create interest and respect between two or more people. In a selling situation, you want to create rapport and then bond as quickly as possible. There's more about Bonding and Rapport in Chapter 9.

> The problem with traditional selling systems is that the prospect can run from one end of the submarine to the other, in and out of compartments, and the salesperson is forced to chase the prospect.

When Selling, Go for the Top

On a call, don't ask to see someone far down the pecking order just to play it safe. Here's how a Sandler President's Club member got a sale after asking to see the chief executive of a large insurance agency:

"Approaching the switchboard operator, I asked for the chief executive. The receptionist showed me to the bank of elevators, and before I realized it, I was standing in the president's office on the fifty-third floor. I began the selling system, and before long the president said, 'Based on the questions you're asking me, the man you want to see is our vice president of sales.'

"Without missing a beat, I said, 'Thanks. I don't suppose you'd take me down to introduce me to him, would you?' (This technique is called the Dummy Curve, and you'll learn how to use it in Chapter 6.)

"The president got up from behind his desk and walked me to the office of the vice president of sales, who had a very surprised look on his face when we entered the room. 'Fred,' the president said to his VP, 'see if this fellow has anything we can use.' And with that, the president left me alone with the VP.

"Not really knowing who I was—was I a stranger, or the president's brother-in-law?—the vice president of sales quickly became an attentive prospect. The sale was closed that morning!"

This student might have closed the sale anyway, but there's a good chance he would have worked a lot harder had he not had the courage to break the rules and ask to see the chief executive. It certainly would have been more difficult working up to the vice president of sales than going down. This student turned a cold call into a referred lead in a matter of minutes—a referred lead with lots of clout!

Once you've established rapport, you leave that compartment and move into Up-Front Contracting, which includes the compartments of Pain (see Chapter 11), Budget (Chapter 12), and Decision (Chapter 13). During this step, you make an agreement with the prospect about what's going to occur during the sales process, and once the agreement is firm, the pressure is off because the sale is closed.

Essentially, your Up-Front Contract says to the prospect: "If you have 'pain' (in other words, a need or a want), and you agree that I can fix it, you will spend the money to get rid of the 'pain.' Furthermore, you're the person who can make the decision to spend the money."

It's simple! However, this step is time-consuming. Even if the prospect agrees to the Up-Front Contract, it may not be valid. Remember, prospects lie! They've been taught to lie to salespeople. In a prospect's Golden Rule book, it's not a sin to mislead a salesperson. Therefore, it's important for you to spend some extra time in this compartment before you seal it and move forward. In Chapter 10, I'll explain more about the Up-Front Contract, along with the techniques you can use to validate it.

Next compartment: Fulfillment. All you've got to do now is fulfill your Up-Front Contract. Do what you agreed to do. Demonstrate to your prospects that your product or service will make their pain go away. Using the Sandler Selling System, you examine some, or perhaps all, of the pains expressed by the prospect. Every so often you take the prospect's temperature (a technique that I'll discuss in Chapter 14) to determine how close the prospect is to realizing that the sale is closed. At some point during this step, your prospects become convinced that they should buy your product or service.

Live a Straight Life in an Unstraight World and . . . You're Going to Get Killed!

Many salespeople fail in our profession because they can't overcome their negative view of the word *manipulation*.

These people believe that manipulation violates their value system, when, in fact, *manipulation* is not a dirty word. *Webster's* says that to be *manipulative* means (1) "to work or handle skillfully" or (2) "to manage artfully or shrewdly; often in an unfair way." Note that it doesn't say always in an unfair way. Manipulation does not mean that you have to lie, cheat, or deceive. Manipulation is part of the selling game, and believe me, prospects know it!

Society accepts manipulation from a variety of professions—selling, law, and psychiatry, to name three. You wouldn't want a lawyer representing you to adhere to the principle of "foolish honesty." You might not even be ready to have your therapist tell you everything.

Then again, if all prospects were straight all the time, there probably would be a good case for full disclosure. But in the real world, prospects have learned the best way to gain the advantage over a salesperson is through manipulation:

> "I don't like to discuss budget. Why don't you give me your best price?"
> "You're looking good, but I really can't promise anything. Can you drop your price a bit?"
> "If you leave it for a few days, maybe we can try it out. That would go a long way toward helping us make a decision."

Prospects are using these types of manipulative moves on you all the time. The next time you feel guilty about a particular selling technique you feel to be manipulative, consider the following: as soon as you find a straight prospect, go straight! Chances are they are few and far between, if you can find one at all.

Finally, you wrap it up in the Post-Sell compartment. To protect yourself from Buyer 's Remorse, you revalidate your agreement. You want to avoid getting a sale and then later receiving a message from your new customer that says, "Please hold up. I've got a problem." The Post-Sell, which is the topic of Chapter 15, is further assurance that you've actually got a sale.

These steps, covering all the compartments of the submarine, make up the basic theory of the Sandler Selling System. I won't tell you that the system is as easy to master as it reads. It's a new experience in selling. One of the reasons it works so well is because it keeps the prospect off balance! Using the Sandler Selling System, you're going to show prospects some techniques they've never seen before. As a result, you'll control your sales calls, and you'll have fun doing it. However, you've got to practice the system, and the techniques that I explain in the following chapters, to make it part of your personality and to master it. *Remember:* You can't teach a kid to ride a bike at a seminar.

6

WHAT YOU KNOW CAN HURT YOU, SO DUMMY UP!

Sell today and educate tomorrow.

—DAVID H. SANDLER

L ike any other submarine, the Sandler Submarine is powered by fuel, or in this case, techniques. Before I explain each step of the Sandler Selling System to you, I want to share with you several techniques that you can use to gracefully move through each compartment of the submarine. These techniques have been developed by Sandler Training, and to succeed with the Sandler Selling System, it will be important to learn these techniques, experiment with them, and practice them. When you master the techniques, and you pay attention to the details that follow, you're going to have fun with your sales career. And then, you're going to make more money than you ever thought was possible!

The next three chapters are devoted to techniques. To begin, let me tell you about the Dummy Curve.

"Why don't you put together a proposal to explain how we might be able to best use your product in our company?"

You've heard that one before from prospects, haven't you?

Or how about these:

> "I'm not sure we're going to do anything right now, but why
> don't you go ahead and give me your best price?"
> "I like your proposal, but why don't we try a 30-day trial before
> we commit to the full package?"
> "Could you give us more clarification about how you would
> implement your service, in writing?"

These statements are all part of the selling dance that I explained in Chapter 1. The prospect's role is to gather as much information as possible, negotiate the best possible price, and give up nothing. Prospects instinctively run to this agenda anytime they're face-to-face with a salesperson. Through the years, prospects have learned, at the mercy of the sales profession, that they can usually get what they want from a desperate salesperson.

Dummy Up and Sell More!

Here are a few "dummy-up" phrases to incorporate into your sales vocabulary:

> "I forgot . . ."
> "Let me see if I have this straight . . ."
> "I don't understand . . ."
> "Help me with . . ."
> "Tell me more about . . ."
> "Did you mean . . ."
> "I don't suppose . . ."

Here are some suggestions of how to use the dummy-up technique:

> "I've forgotten, Ron, did you say delivery was important to you?" (The salesperson knows what Ron said about delivery, and since the delivery dates are in the salesperson's favor, he uses the dummy-up technique to reinforce his position.)

> "Sharon, I don't understand what you mean when you say you need to know more about the clauses in the agreement. Can you help me with that?" (This salesperson is guarding against mind reading. The dummy-up technique helps the salesperson gather more information and invites the prospect to continue talking.)

> "We talked about whether or not you had a budget set aside for this—didn't we?" (Budget was covered in the first meeting between the salesperson and the prospect. Now, the salesperson uses the dummy-up technique to nail down specific dollars.)

There are many more phrases that you can develop on your own. The important point is to encourage you to find some dummy-up phrases that you're comfortable using. Then, get to work!

Why do prospects behave this way? As I explained earlier, it's a defensive reaction. They don't trust sales professionals. They figure the salesperson is lying to them, so it's OK if they lie too. However, there's more to it than that. The prospect wants to know what *you* know. The prospect knows that your product or service has the capability of improving productivity and/or lowering costs. You bring something of value to the marketplace, and the prospect is wise enough to realize it. The trick for the prospect, however, is to get you to spill the beans without paying you for the privilege.

Prospects who extract all you know about your product or service, along with your best price, can then beat up their current suppliers, including your competition. They need your numbers so they can go to your competition and say, "I have a better deal than what you're giving me. What will you do about it?" And believe it or not, the world is full of amateur salespeople who are satisfying these needs. What they're really doing is corrupting the marketplace!

In an earlier chapter I called this phenomenon "unpaid consulting," and as a professional, you want to protect yourself from it. The problem is that traditional selling turns you into an unpaid consultant. Under the guise of doing a "little extra work" to get the sale, you end up working for nothing. Therefore, what you know really can hurt you, especially if you fall prey to your prospect's system instead of following your own.

Today, right now, I urge you to set some new goals for yourself as a sales professional. Begin with this one: *Get information. Don't give it.*

When was the Battle of Hastings?

Do you know the answer? Did you hear yourself thinking it? I've asked that question countless times in front of audiences of salespeople, and, without fail, someone shouts out: "Ten sixty-six!" That person carried around that piece of knowledge for years, perhaps since elementary school. I always ask, "When was the last time you got paid for knowing that answer?" The response is always, "Never."

Exactly. Which leads me to the next new goal that I urge you to set for yourself: *Sell today and educate tomorrow.*

That's a difficult rule to learn and follow. As a sales professional, you may like to educate. After all, that's your business. But educating your prospect before the sale may not result in a new customer or client. And since you probably spent years learning about your product or service, not to mention years of labor to master your selling system, when someone asks you a question, you can't wait to give him the answer. Don't do it. *Sell today and educate tomorrow.*

> Salespeople who don't feel OK about themselves are even more likely to give away the store.

It doesn't matter whether you're an accountant, an engineer, a lawyer, banker, doctor, consultant, or any other professional. You've invested time, money, and energy in your profession. You deserve to get paid for what you know! However, the natural tendency is for you to spill your candy in the lobby. You can't get paid that way. So let's form an Up-Front Contract between you and me. I agree that it's going to be difficult for you to resist educating your prospects; and you agree to remain open-minded about what I have to tell you so that you won't fight these new ideas. If that's acceptable to you, let's move on.

Why are salespeople so quick to give away information? I said earlier that it's a natural tendency for salespeople to want to educate. That's true, but more important, they don't want to look stupid. Salespeople who don't feel OK about themselves are even more likely to give away the store. They're easy targets for prospects to turn them into unpaid consultants.

The fact of the matter is, uneducated salespeople are frequently more successful than veterans. Neophytes can't help looking like dummies, but then, the smarter they get, the worse off they become. Consider this typical scenario that occurs every week in sales organizations across the country:

Joe is a new salesperson. When he arrives on the scene, he's given a brief introduction about the company's products and services. After all, from the company's point of view, there's no sense investing too much time in Joe until he proves himself. When Joe meets with a prospect, he's uncomfortable about his lack of product knowledge, and therefore, he does very little talking. As a result, the prospect talks three-fourths of the time, and Joe speaks very little. At this stage of Joe's development, he's a "dummy," although no one's going to say that to him.

For Joe's first assignment, he's handed a long list of "dead" accounts. The company doesn't tell him the status of these accounts, but the company's veteran sales pros have already called on these accounts and they've gotten nowhere. So the company hands the list to Joe, figuring that he can't do any harm with them.

Not knowing any better, and being the dummy that he is, Joe begins making sales calls. He runs into some irate prospects—"I told you people already that I'm not interested in your product"—but that makes no difference to Joe. He's got something to prove. He continues charging ahead, and eventually he stumbles into the office of an inactive customer who proclaims: "Where have you been all these years? I need your service!"

Proudly, Joe takes the order, then dashes back to his office, where he shouts out: "I got one!"

"How? From whom?" shouts Joe's startled sales manager.

Joe has no idea that no one expected him to close a sale, but it doesn't matter. He's thrilled to have bumped into a buyer. Everyone congratulates him, and the manager grabs the new account and immediately assigns it to a veteran in the office. Meanwhile, the dummy is sent back to the wolves with cries of encouragement to "go get another one."

He does! Again and again, Joe scores a victory in the field. And then one day, look what happens to him. Joe says to himself, "If I am this successful knowing nothing, how much more successful could I be if I got smart about my product?" When he shares his thoughts with his sales manager, the company decides to invest in Joe. He's sent to an intensive training program to learn all there is to know about his product. Soon, Joe believes he knows it all, and now look what happens: he can't wait to tell the world!

Unfortunately for Joe, he's no longer a dummy. He's now an amateur. He wasn't performing all that badly as a dummy, but watch what happens to him after his transformation.

Don't Paint Seagulls in Your Prospect's Picture!

Let me tell you a story about eight-year-old Nancy, a student in the public school system. One day during art class, Nancy painted a picture. Considering her age and development as a young artist, the picture of a house and the setting sun was really quite good. However, it was obvious that the picture was unbalanced. Nancy had painted the house and the sun to the left side of the canvas.

Nancy's art teacher, who held a master's degree in art, observed the picture and said, "Nancy, this is really a fine painting. But it needs something on this right side." And with that, the teacher picked up a brush and painted a seagull in the upper right corner of the canvas. Nancy became very upset and began to cry.

That evening at the dinner table, Nancy was still upset. Her father asked, "What's the trouble, Nancy?" The little girl replied, "Nothing," but her pouting face encouraged her father to continue pressing the issue. Finally, Nancy showed her father the painting. He admired it and said enthusiastically, "This is very good, Nancy. I really like the seagull." At that, Nancy burst into tears and ran off to her bedroom.

After Nancy's father learned that the seagull was the source of her unhappiness, he complained to the art teacher, who in her own defense cited her reasoning and her credentials. Getting nowhere with the teacher, Nancy's father visited the school principal, and then contacted his attorney. One battle followed another, and eventually both parties ended up in court. It was a long drawn out trial with many hours of testimony about freedom of expression, the role of an educator, and so on.

Having listened intently as both sides told their stories, the judge turned to Nancy and asked why she had become so upset about the seagull. Nancy replied, "Because I did not see it there."

Case closed; decision in favor of Nancy.

So what's a seagull have to do with selling?

Your prospects have a mental picture of their needs even before they meet you. Every change or addition you make to their picture may cause the prospects to become uncomfortable, even unhappy, like Nancy. If it's necessary to make a change in a prospect's mental picture, you'll be wise to let the prospect "discover" the need for the change.

You might think that certain features or benefits of your product or service would help you close a sale if only your prospect knew about the features or benefits. But it would be a mistake to paint a seagull in your prospect's picture.

Instead, dummy up. Ask a few questions to find out if your prospect would like a "seagull" in his picture. If so, all to your advantage. If not, no damage done.

Back in the field, a prospect asks Joe if his product will do "such and such." As a dummy, Joe would have said, "Gosh, I don't know. Let me call someone at the office and find out." But now when he's asked the same question, Joe knows all the answers. "Will it *do* such and such?" he says to the prospect. "Let me tell you all about it." And from that point on, his mouth can't be stopped. He gives away the store. He spills the candy. He tells all. And he gets nothing in return. Joe used to *help* his prospects close the sale, but ever since his intensive training, all he does is share the information.

What's happened to Joe? Obviously, he talks too much. When he meets his prospects, he talks 70 percent of the time. The prospects are lucky to get to talk 30 percent of the time. It used to be the other way around. Consequently, his closing ratio dropped dramatically, but he can't figure out what's wrong.

What's wrong is simply this: Joe is no longer a dummy. He's an *amateur,* and as an amateur, he's unaware of an important fact. During a sales call, his job is to gather information, not give it away. Instead of talking so much and sharing his extensive knowledge, Joe should dummy up and invite his prospects to share their pain about their needs and desires. As long as Joe continues to do most of the talking, his prospects have no opportunity to paint a picture of what they want and what they're willing to buy.

One of two things will now happen to Joe:

1. He will continue as an amateur, but he will probably get fired for lack of performance. He'll then move on to another sales job,

where he'll perform equally as badly. If he finds a job that isn't too demanding, he'll stick with it, but he'll never set the world on fire, and he'll do nothing to help advance the profession of selling. Hopefully, if he's going to remain an amateur, he'll give up sales altogether and find another career.

2. Or Joe could advance to the professional ranks of selling. How so? Simply by becoming a dummy again on purpose. If he does so, his prospects will begin talking 70 percent of the time, and he'll talk 30 percent or less. He'll be able to lead his prospects step-by-step through the selling process, or the compartments of the Sandler Submarine that were listed in Chapter 5, and his prospects will never realize what's happening. He'll become more successful than he ever imagined.

The difference between Joe the amateur and Joe the professional is that the amateur sometimes does the right thing, but he doesn't know when or why; the professional always does the right thing, and he always knows when and why.

If you want to become more successful in sales, then dummy up and become a professional.

Dummy-Up Responses for Three Typical Objections

PROSPECT: *How long have you been in business?*

SALESPERSON: *That's an interesting question. . . . You must have asked that for a reason.*

PROSPECT: *Is it guaranteed?*

SALESPERSON: *Supposing I said it was? What happens next? [Pause] Supposing I said it wasn't?*

PROSPECT: *It's more than we want to spend.*

SALESPERSON: *That's not unusual. Off the record, how much were you hoping it would be?*

PROSPECT: *[Replies with a number.]*

SALESPERSON: *That's it?*

PROSPECT: *That's it.*

SALESPERSON: *So fixing your problem isn't that important?*

PROSPECT: *Sure it is.*

SALESPERSON: *Which part do you want to fix?*

The most famous dummy of all time has to be TV's Lieutenant Columbo, a pop-culture icon from the 1970s with no known first name. As played by the actor Peter Falk, Columbo may be, after Sherlock Holmes, the most celebrated fictional detective in history. Why? Columbo made the dummy fashionable.

Remember how, halfway out the door, he would reenter the room to ask the suspect just one more dumb question? And who could forget his dress and behavior? The well-worn trench coat. The hand-to-his-head movement that helped him look a little slow. His obsessive note-taking. The constant struggle to make sense of anything. Columbo planned it all, of course, to lower his suspects' guard. Consequently, the suspects always spoke more frankly. After all, they figured, what would it hurt? What could this dummy do with their information? But after a series of deceptively dumb questions, the detective always caught the guilty party. No wrongdoer ever escaped Columbo, the most successful dummy of all.

Imagine Columbo as a salesperson. See him sitting in front of a prospect, and watch how he responds:

PROSPECT: *Your competition is cheaper than you.*

COLUMBO: *Looks like I won't be getting your business then, huh?*

PROSPECT: *I haven't placed an order with your company in 10 years.*

COLUMBO: *Let me ask you this. What am I doing here?*

PROSPECT: *When can we get started?*

COLUMBO: *Don't know. Let me call the office and see if someone down there knows when we have an opening.*

At every step, Columbo dummies up and struggles with his response. Chances are, that's going to be hard for you to do. No one wants to look foolish in front of a prospect. It goes against the grain, doesn't it? But go ahead, Start to struggle a little. After all, selling is merely acting. If you try it—realizing that it takes practice to perfect the Dummy Curve technique—you'll soon discover that selling is not only more enjoyable but more profitable too!

SANDLER SELLING TIP

The professional does what he did as a dummy, on purpose.
David Sandler taught his students never to ask a question, make a statement, or behave in any way unless it was in their best interest to do so. He also taught that the best sales discussion is one in which the prospect does most of the talking. These two guidelines can, at first, seem difficult to implement, especially for people who are used to dominating the conversation and spouting endless product knowledge! Start simple. Before your next meeting, use the Internet to do a little homework (not a lot), so that you are ready to ask some intelligent questions about the prospect, his or her company, the market, and so on. The goal is to make this discussion about the other person and his needs, not about you and your company.

—DHM

CAN ASKING QUESTIONS BE THE ANSWER?

If you want to escape the traps of

traditional selling and surpass your

best performances of the past, learn

the Reversing technique as soon as

possible. When you do, you'll stop

telling and you'll start selling.

—DAVID H. SANDLER

One of the things people say they like least about salespeople is that they talk too much. And it's true. I've discovered that if you talk less, you'll sell more, and that's a rule you can take to the bank.

Again, traditional sales trainers have created a problem. They believe you can talk a prospect into a sale. I don't agree. In their efforts to do the right thing, traditionally trained salespeople talk 70 percent of the time in front of a prospect when they ought to talk less than 30 percent of the time. The problem is, they don't know how to get the prospect to do most of the talking. They can't talk less because they can't stand the silence.

Talking less isn't an issue when using the Sandler Selling System. You can keep the sales meeting moving by asking questions, or Reversing the prospect. Reversing is the best way to utilize the Dummy Curve technique explained in the previous chapter. It's a way to "present" information, rather than "tell it" to a prospect. Also, it helps the salesperson uncover the prospect's pain.

Have you ever noticed that people rarely reveal their true intentions up front? We've all been programmed to cover up, especially in front of a salesperson. It's a form of protection. By not saying what's really on our mind, we have an opportunity to gather information, to "test the waters," to "check out the territory," before we reveal our true intentions or make a commitment. You've done it many times, no doubt, and it's being done back to you all the time.

> Traditionally trained salespeople talk 70 percent of the time in front of a prospect when they ought to talk less than 30 percent of the time.

Husbands and wives play this game all the time. See if this sounds familiar:

HUSBAND *(who wants to go to the movies):* *I'm home, sweetheart. Hey, a friend at work was telling me that Big New Hollywood Blockbuster is a great movie.*

WIFE *(who doesn't want to go to the movies):* *Oh, yes, I heard a review on the TODAY show. They said it was wonderful too.*

HUSBAND *(thinking he might be going to the movie tonight, but still uncertain):* *Well, maybe we'll get to see it sometime soon.*

WIFE: *Sure, honey, maybe we will.*

HUSBAND *(now feeling safe):* *How about tonight?*

WIFE: *Well, I'm a little tired. I don't feel like going out tonight.*

HUSBAND *(protecting himself):* *Me neither. Maybe we'll go on the weekend.*

No one got hurt in this scenario, but the husband wasn't totally honest either.

Here's how it works in a sales scenario:

PROSPECT: *Will this software package work with Windows?*

AMATEUR SALESPERSON *(excited at sensing a sale!):* *Why, yes!*

PROSPECT: *Even the latest update?*

SALESPERSON: *Yes, even the latest update.*

PROSPECT: *Well, all the other programs I've tried to run with that version haven't been successful.*

Wham! The salesperson just got clobbered by an iceberg. Picture an iceberg in your mind's eye. All you see above the surface of the water is a small chunk, right? The rest of the iceberg, the part that will do the most damage, is 20 feet under the water and out of sight. Prospects tend to let you see only the tip of the iceberg. And unless you know better, you're likely to get clobbered. Our software salesperson is now forced to recover, if he can.

But why did he create all that pressure for himself? How much easier it would have been had he uncovered the prospect's true intentions before boxing himself in with his enthusiastic responses.

How Does Reversing Help You?

1. By asking questions, you get the prospect to do most of the talking.
2. Questions shift the focus from you to the prospect, where it belongs.
3. Questions flatter the prospect and show your interest.
4. Questions help the prospect resolve objections. Some people need to speak out loud to make sense of a situation.
5. Questions help you gather information, which leads to more questions.
6. Questions probe. They uncover the real issues. Prospects hide their true motives as a built-in defense mechanism to thwart salespeople. Questions, when handled in a nurturing manner, help the prospect reveal true motives without any pressure from you!
7. Questions keep you from getting boxed in by a prospect's response.
8. Questions allow the prospect to become emotionally involved. People make decisions intellectually, but they buy emotionally.
9. Questions keep you from contracting the most dreaded illness of amateur salespeople: diarrhea of the mouth!
10. Questions help you gain credibility in the eyes of the prospect. Amateur salespeople frequently spend their time promising more than they can deliver. This doesn't happen when you're asking questions.
11. Questions help prospects solve their own objections. Only one person has the know-how and the wherewithal to solve the prospect's objections. And that's the prospect!
12. Questions enable you to obtain information that otherwise wouldn't be forthcoming.

Look at how Reversing would have helped the salesperson in the above scenario:

PROSPECT: *Will this software package work with Windows?*

PROFESSIONAL SALESPERSON: *That's an interesting question. Why do you ask?*

PROSPECT: *I'm wondering just how difficult it will be to run in Windows.*

PROFESSIONAL SALESPERSON: *That makes sense. But can I ask why that's important to you?*

PROSPECT: *Because all other programs I've tried to run in the latest update haven't worked easily.*

Notice how the pro gently reversed the prospect into revealing the *one* issue that mattered most? The professional salesperson can now either respond to the prospect's concern, or move the prospect to a software package that doesn't require the problematic operating system.

The other advantage of the Reversing technique is that it keeps the focus of the meeting on the prospect, where it belongs. The prospect doesn't feel any pressure and therefore has no reason to be fearful of the salesperson.

Once a prospect gets emotionally involved in a sales meeting, the reverses go unnoticed. However, you've got to be careful to keep your reverses from sounding harsh or arrogant. A softening statement preceding the reverse decreases the pressure on the prospect, keeps the prospect from becoming defensive, and encourages a "straight" response.

Some examples of softening expressions include these: "Good question," "I'm glad you asked me that," "That's a good point," and "That must be an important question to you."

Your tone of voice is also important while reversing. Remember as a kid how you feared the neighbor's big dog? When you went into your neighbor's yard, how did you speak to the dog? You probably used a soft tone of voice as you said, "Easy, boy. Good doggy." Well, the same principle applies in reversing. Speak softly. Nice and easy. Be careful not to frighten your prospect. I suggest you pretend you're standing in front of the neighbor's dog when you reverse with your prospects.

Here are some typical sales situations, followed by an appropriate reverse. Commit these to memory, and you'll be well on your way to using this powerful technique.

Testing the Water

SALESPERSON: *I get the feeling that you [fill in the blank]. Is that a fair statement?*

PROSPECT: *Yes.*

SALESPERSON: *Fine.*

Or

PROSPECT: *No.*

SALESPERSON: *What is a fair statement?*

Controlling the Interview

Use this reverse when the prospect is taking control of the sales meeting and you want to slow down the process:

SALESPERSON: *That's an interesting point. But you're on page 7 and I'm still on page 3. Could we just back up for a moment?*

Pressure-Packed Moments

Sometimes the prospect will bear down on you. When it happens, here's the appropriate reverse:

SALESPERSON: *Ms. Brown, why are you putting all this pressure on me?*

This is a reverse that works in reverse. You sense your prospect is feeling pressure, so you say: "I feel pressure right now, but I'm not sure why."

Situations You Can't Handle

If faced with a situation that you can't handle, try this reverse:

SALESPERSON: *We have a problem.*

When the prospect asks what the problem is, you outline the problem, and then you say: "Do you see a way to overcome this problem?"

Never Answer an Unasked Question

Sometimes what sounds like a question is actually just a statement. For example, the prospect says: "The price is too high." That's a statement, not a question. In this form, it doesn't call for an answer, although most salespeople will answer it. The statement is obviously designed to pressure the salesperson, and the prospect is looking for a response. You can shift the pressure back to the prospect by helping the prospect convert the statement into a question:

PROSPECT: *The price is too high.*

SALESPERSON: *Which means . . . ?*

Here are some variations of the same issue:

PROSPECT: *Your deliveries are too slow.*

SALESPERSON: *And . . .?*

PROSPECT: *You people always do this to me.*

SALESPERSON: *"Do this to me" means . . .?*

PROSPECT: *I'm really unhappy about this situation.*

SALESPERSON: *When you say "unhappy," George, what does that mean?*

PROSPECT: *I think this problem should be settled.*

SALESPERSON: *"Settled" means . . .?*

There's no way for you to know how to answer comments like "The price is too high." Traditionally, a salesperson has been trained to say, "How high?" But by doing so, you're implying that there's validity to the prospect's comment. Remember, there's a difference between reporting and objecting. *Reporting* that "the price is too high" may be the prospect's way of dealing with stress, and it may not necessarily be an invitation to negotiate the price. *Objecting* to the price means the prospect may want to negotiate. For example:

PROSPECT *(reporting): Charlie, your price is too high.*

SALESPERSON: *Which means . . . ?*

PROSPECT: *Which means we're going to have to talk about lowering your price if you want my business.*

You cannot be sure what the prospect is thinking unless you use the reverse.

Here are some additional Reversing strategies.

The Magic Wand Reverse

Use this reverse to help your prospects paint pictures of their wants and needs. You say: "Sarah, if you had a magic wand that could produce the ideal solution to your problem, what would it be?" Then, step out of the way and let the prospect paint the picture. Similarly, there's the Druthers Reverse. "If you had your druthers, Sarah . . ."

The "You Start" Reverse

This is a good technique to help the prospect open up:

SALESPERSON: *Mary, we need to discuss all aspects of your problem. Is this a fair statement?*

PROSPECT: *Yes.*

SALESPERSON: *Fine. You start.*

The Off-the-Record Reverse

Another reverse that will invite the prospect to open up goes like this: "Bill, off the record, what price are you looking for?" Obviously the answer won't be off the record, but it will relieve a lot of pressure, and many times it will get the prospect to reveal more than you imagined.

The Change-of-Pace Reverse

Sometimes, to change the pace of your reversing pattern, you should answer the question and then immediately reverse:

PROSPECT: *Does this come in blue?*

SALESPERSON: *Sure. Let me ask you this, why is blue of interest to you?*

That's not as good as a normal reverse, but it does change the pace, and it's safe to use if it won't box you in.

The following reverses are designed to keep a sales meeting in motion:

> "Let me see if I have this straight."
> "I don't understand. Tell me more about that." "I'm not sure.
>   What do you think?"
> "Help me with that. What does that mean?"
> "Why is that a problem?"
> "There must be a reason you feel that way."

Handling Stalls and Objections

There's only one person who's qualified to handle a prospect's stalls and objections, and it's *not* the salesperson. It's the prospect. If stalls and objections frequently come up in your sales calls, it's a good idea to bring them up *before* the prospect has the opportunity. If you bring them up first, several good things happen:

- It helps your credibility when the prospect sees that you're not afraid to bring up stalls and objections, even before you're asked. This promotes a feeling of trust.
- You remain in control, not the prospect.
- You can save time and get down to business faster, easier.

Here's how you can handle stalls and objections up front: "Art, sometimes when I talk to people about what we do—and it may not be the case here—sometimes they tell me one of the following: They see all vendors as being the same; they hate the idea of going through the process of whom to select to provide this product [or service]; they had a bad experience the last time they tried someone new; or they're not sure which direction or application will be best for them. Which of these, if any, Art, is a concern to you?"

The idea is to take three or four of the most common objections—those that you hear most often—and phrase them in a multiple-choice question that prompts the prospect to select one or more. This technique smokes out an objection that might get in the way of your progress later in the presentation.

When your prospect selects one of the objections, you then reverse by saying:

"Really? I'm surprised by your answer. Why did you pick that one?"

Probe a couple of more times to find out the real objection. Then, decide if the prospect's objection will be a problem or if you can handle it later in the presentation.

Another variation of this reverse becomes helpful when you hear the prospect raise an objection. For example:

PROSPECT: *Well, that's just too much money.*

SALESPERSON: *Let me tell you what I hear when you say that.*

Or

> *People generally say that for a number of reasons. (List multiple reasons, then reverse by saying:) Which one of these, if any, explains your comment?*

The Exception to Reversing

There's an exception to the Reversing Rule. If a prospect asks the identical question twice, answer it!

PROSPECT: *How much is it?*

SALESPERSON: *Good question. Why do you ask?*

PROSPECT: *How much is it?*

Don't antagonize the prospect. Answer the question. However, it's rare that a prospect will ask an identical question twice.

When prospects hear the reverse, they don't know what it is, so they tend to think their question was unclear. Consequently, they'll generally rephrase the question.

The Stroke-Repeat-Reverse Technique

Never forget that a prospect is suspicious of a salesperson. Prospects are crafty. They've got their own arsenal of techniques to use on salespeople, and some are better than others. Almost all prospects will use "play-it-safe" words or phrases, including these:

> "You're close."
> "All things being equal, . . ."
> "Apples for apples . . ."

When a prospect wants to play it safe, the best way to respond is to use the Stroke-Repeat-Reverse technique, which sounds like this:

SALESPERSON: *Thanks, Fred. I appreciate (there's the stroke) the fact that you're telling me I'm close (there's the repeat), but let me ask you a question (the reverse).*

Here's another example:

PROSPECT: *I feel, in view of all you have said and done, there's a good chance we can do business with your company.*

(What does that mean? Unless you're a mind reader, who knows?)

SALESPERSON: *And that business will be appreciated, too, Tom (the stroke). When you say "good chance" (repeat), let me ask you, what does that mean?*

PROSPECT: *Well, we really like you, Rich, and we're giving you top consideration.*

(What does "top consideration" mean? Again, who knows?)

SALESPERSON: *Thank you, Tom. Let me ask you another question. When you say "top consideration," what does that mean, exactly?*

Here are a few more play-it-safe words. You'll recognize them because they've been stringing you along for years:

Might	Maybe
Possible	Considering
Opportunity	Look into
Try	It appears
Don't worry about it	If I have my way
Looks good	

All of these words are meaningless. So when you hear them, use your Reversing skills to clarify them.

Perhaps the Reversing technique feels a little foreign to you, but I assure you that you've experienced it before. Every time you visit a doctor, you spend the first several minutes responding to reverses. Doctors are the greatest practitioners of Reversing.

Let's say you go the doctor with a sore shoulder. The doctor listens to your complaint, and then does what? Asks questions, of course. In fact, the doctor will ask a series of probing questions, such as: "How long have you been in pain?" "Where does it hurt?" "Is the pain sharp or dull?" "What happens if you move your arm this way, or that way?"

The doctor doesn't rush in to solve your problem. Nor does the doctor give you a dissertation about the anatomy of the body. Certainly, at this point, the doctor doesn't gather up a collection of slides, flipcharts, brochures, and so on, to show you all the different varieties of shoulders in the human race!

> Every time you visit a doctor, you spend the first several minutes responding to reverses.

Before "closing" you, the doctor probes to discover precisely what's wrong. Only then can the doctor help you. Only after a thorough examination can the doctor make a decision that will, hopefully, relieve your pain. If the doctor acted any differently, you'd begin to worry, wouldn't you? You might even start looking for another doctor.

So why shouldn't you, as a sales professional, behave similarly? Why shouldn't you ask questions? Why shouldn't you clarify the meaning of words? Why not get all the details before you make a commitment?

The No-Pressure Reversing Exercise

The use of this exercise breaks the boredom of the day-to-day routine in the office *and* helps a group of salespeople learn the Reversing technique.

Here's what you do:

Get a silver dollar and give it to one of your salespeople. Tell him to put the coin in his pocket. The rule is that whenever this salesperson is asked a question during the week, he has to answer with a reverse. If he doesn't reverse, he has to surrender the coin to the person who asked him the question.

The salesperson who possesses the coin at the end of the week wins a prize.

During this exercise, every question should be reversed. Even simple questions like "What time is it?" should be reversed with "Good question. Why do you ask?" This no-pressure exercise is a great way for everyone on the sales team to learn the Reversing skill.

SANDLER SELLING TIP

No power trips. Don't make the mistake of thinking that Reversing means proving the prospect wrong or intimidating the prospect into agreeing with anything you say. If Reversing ever begins to erode the goodwill you've built up in the relationship, if your questions ever begin to undermine your ongoing Bonding and Rapport with the prospect, that's not Reversing. It's a power trip. ("Hi, Jim, thanks for coming in to meet with us. How are you today?" "That's a fascinating question. I assume you asked it for a reason?")   —DHM

The use of the reverse is an ideal technique to help you act like a pro. If you want to escape the traps of traditional selling and surpass your best performances of the past, learn the Reversing technique as soon as possible. When you do, you'll stop *telling* and you'll start *selling*. Like the doctor, the tool of your trade is asking questions—reversing— to gather information that will help you successfully close the sale.

Now let me ask you a question: Do you think asking questions can be the answer to more sales?

8

NEGATIVE REVERSE SELLING®: THE MOST POTENT SALES TECHNIQUE OF ALL

Using this technique creates an environment in which the prospect sells the salesperson. Once you master Negative Reverse Selling, you can sit back and watch your prospects sell you on wanting whatever it is you're selling.

—DAVID H. SANDLER

I need to tell you a story about two fishermen.

Two men were out fishing one day; one was a professional, the other was an amateur. The professional, as you would expect, knew exactly where to go fishing to catch the most fish. He knew when the fish would be biting, and as a result, he always came home with a string of fish. The amateur, on the other hand, wasn't very successful. He'd drop his line in the water without any planning. He'd pull it up, drop it again, and seldom would he catch a fish. Most of the time, he merely managed to lose his bait. As you can imagine, fishing wasn't much fun for the amateur, but the professional fisherman could never get enough of it.

The professional had observed the amateur on this particular day, and after filling his bucket with fish, he struck up a conversation with the neophyte.

"Looks like you're not having a good day," said the pro.

"You're right. As a matter of fact," responded the amateur, "I can't seem to hook anything, even when I get a nibble."

"Well, maybe you're working too hard. Let's see what you're doing. Let me ask you this: What causes you to pull your fishing line up in the first place?"

"I get a nibble," said the amateur, a bit sarcastically. "OK, you get a nibble. Then what?" pursued the pro.

"I pull up my line, and there's nothing on it. Most of the time, the bait is gone."

The pro hesitated for a moment and then continued. "When you feel the tug on your fishing line, do you have any idea what's really happening?"

"Why, no, I never thought about it."

"The fish is killing the bait," the pro explained. "He has yet to take a bite out of it. He's just killing it. He might whack it with his tail. If you pull up the line at this point, all you'll have is dead bait, if anything. Make sense? You've got to have respect for that fish and his eating habits. The fish is going to kill the bait before he bites."

"So when he kills it, he's got nothing to do but eat it, right?" asked the amateur, now completely attentive to the pro.

"Well, you're close. You see, it takes the fish a couple of seconds to kill the bait, and by this time, all the fish in the neighborhood swim over to the action. They gather around, and they want some of the bait too. Why do you think that's so?"

"I guess because they're hungry."

"You're right," says the pro. "Would you like to eat your meal in the midst of a hundred hungry people?"

"No."

"Neither does the fish. So what would you do?"

> The amateur salesperson goes for the close too soon.

"I'd take it and find a place where I could eat alone," answered the amateur.

"And that's exactly what the fish is planning to do, given the chance," continued the pro. "So the next time you get a nibble on your line, instead of yanking that rod, I suggest you strip a little line off your reel. Give the line a little slack. Let the fish take it. Think about this fish looking for a place to eat its catch. Then, as soon as the line tightens up that's when you set your hook. Got it?"

The next time the amateur felt a nibble on his line, he did just what he was told. He gave the fish a little extra line, waited for the line to tighten, and then set the hook. And just as the old pro predicted, he caught the fish.

Now, what can *you* do with this information? Can you catch more fish? Probably. But there's a better payoff for the sales professional. How about using this information to *sell more* and to earn *bigger commissions*?

There's an analogy to be drawn between the amateur salesperson and the amateur fisherman. The amateur salesperson goes for the close too soon. Charging forward and looking aggressive, the amateur salesperson sets the hook prematurely. The result? No sale.

Salespeople who have been trained traditionally are a lot like the amateur fisherman. They can't help losing the sale. They've been taught to set the hook prematurely. Traditionally trained salespeople easily confuse a nibble for a buying signal, and they move in for the kill. But today's prospects are too sophisticated to get hooked by these old selling techniques. Like the fisherman and his fish, the sales professional must respect the buying habits of the prospect.

No High-Pressure Selling!

Despite what most traditional sales trainers tell us, it's very difficult to convince people that they want or need something that they're not already asking to buy. Our experiences have demonstrated that when we try to force-sell our products or services, all we do is evoke feelings of defensiveness in our prospects. Unconsciously, the prospects will "defend" whatever it is they already own or use. Under those circumstances, prospects won't make a "new" decision.

The use of Sandler's Reversing techniques can lead prospects to "discover" that while a previous decision was a wise one, a "new" decision can also be beneficial.

Be patient. Take your prospects through the Pain discussion. Let them "discover" there's a better way—and your product or service is it.

A professional salesperson knows when to close the deal. The pro knows better than to pressure the prospect. People love to buy, but they hate to be sold. Consequently, the professional salesperson leads prospects to close themselves. The salesperson does so by using a technique that I call Negative Reverse Selling.

How does it work? It's simple, really. When the prospect nibbles, the salesperson lets out a little more line. Instead of moving toward the prospect's interest, the salesperson moves away from it. It's the same idea that's used in martial arts. It's the technique of using the momentum of the attacker against the attacker.

Consider this example of Negative Reverse Selling:

PROSPECT: *I think I like what you're saying.*

SALESPERSON: *Interesting. Based on what you have been saying up until now, I would not have guessed you had an interest in my product. What did I miss?*

See the subtle reverse? The loosening of the line? Instead of moving in for what looked like the obvious close, the salesperson gently moved away, all the while setting the hook a little tighter.

Now watch the line tighten up as the prospect responds:

PROSPECT: *Maybe you missed how I see your product solving my problem.*

SALESPERSON: *Great, but I'm still a little confused. Could you tell me more specifically just how you see the fit?*

PROSPECT: *Sure. I'll use it by . . .*

Do you see what's happening? The prospect himself is closing! What could be easier?

To sell like a pro, I suggest you learn to set the hook only when you hear the prospect buy. Even then, one more gentle reverse won't hurt: "Mr. Smith, just what would you like me to do now?" When Mr. Smith speaks, the sale is closed. Now that's exciting!

Stop Handling Stalls and Objections, and Start Reversing

One day I called on a particular company just while I was beginning to develop my Reversing techniques. I got to the end of my presentation, and the prospect said to me, "You know, I really like what you have. But I have a longstanding rule. I never make decisions the first time I see something."

My immediate response was to use this reverse:

"That's not a problem. I also have a longstanding rule. I never come back. Now, what do we do?"

I closed the sale. And that's when I learned to stop handling stalls and objections and to start Reversing!

Negative Reverse Selling consists of two components: the buildup and the takeaway.

Here's an example: "Negative Reverse Selling is a powerful technique, but you won't like it."

The buildup is: "Negative Reverse Selling is a powerful technique." That's the hook.

The takeaway is: "But you won't like it." That's letting out the line.

Using this technique creates an environment in which the prospect sells the salesperson. Once you master Negative Reverse Selling, you can sit back and watch your prospects sell you on wanting whatever it is you're selling. You build up, then take away; build up, then take away . . . and if you do that long enough, your prospects hook themselves.

Why is this technique called Negative Reverse Selling? Because it reverses the process that traditional sales trainers have been teaching for years. In traditional selling, the theory says the burden of closing is the salesperson's responsibility. In other words, as the salesperson, I convince you . . . I persuade you . . . I motivate you to do something that I want you to do.

Negative Reverse Selling says that's all wrong. This powerful technique invites you, as the sales professional, to relax while your prospects carry the burden of doing all the work.

To get into the swing of using Negative Reverse Selling, draw a half-circle on a piece of paper like the illustration in Figure 8.1. Write the numbers 3, 6, and 9 like the time on a clock face (see image 8.1.) Now, draw a horizontal line between the 3 and the 9. Watch what happens.

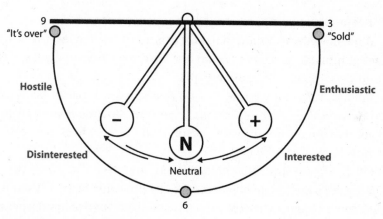

Figure 8.1 *The Pendulum Theory*

Imagine that this clock face stands upright behind a pendulum. In other words, the pendulum swings. The pendulum can move as high as 3 o'clock on one side of the clock, and as high as 9 o'clock in the reverse direction. The pendulum represents your prospect's buying quotient during a selling situation.

At any given time when buyer meets seller, the prospect can be positive, negative, or indifferent to what you're selling. So let's say 3 o'clock represents a positive prospect, 9 o'clock denotes a negative prospect, and 6 o'clock is an indifferent prospect.

Let's assume you've got an indifferent, or neutral, prospect at 6 o'clock. If you can get this prospect's buying quotient to move to 3 o'clock, you've got an enthusiastic and sold prospect. At 5 o'clock, the prospect is getting interested; 4 o'clock, even more interested; but the prospect won't become a customer until the pendulum hits 3. If, however, the pendulum moves to 7 o'clock, your prospect is losing interest; at 8 o'clock, the prospect could become hostile; and at 9 o'clock, you no longer have a prospect.

It's important now to consider one of Newton's laws, which states that a body in motion stays in motion, and a body at rest remains at rest. Combining this principle with Negative Reverse Selling gives you an enormous advantage in every sales meeting.

Let's look at how a traditionally trained salesperson would respond to an enthusiastic prospect who's at 4 o'clock on the Negative Reverse Clock.

The prospect says, "I really like what you have to offer!"

What does the traditionalist do at this point? He moves to 3 o'clock, perches himself on the horizontal line we drew between the 9 and the 3, and says, "Shall I write up the order?"

But as you already know, the 4 o'clock prospect hasn't been sold, and he won't be until he reaches 3. So now, how does the prospect respond to the traditional salesperson who's excited to close the deal? He runs back to a 6 o'clock!

"Well, I'm not sure I'm *that* interested," he says.

Why does the prospect react like that? Pressure. Fear. At this early stage, there's been no trust or rapport established between salesperson and prospect. When the salesperson responds too enthusiastically, the frightened prospect has no choice but to run for protection.

And then what does the traditional salesperson do? He's still up on the horizontal line, and he panics as he sees the prospect slipping away from him. Now he's been trained to show even more enthusiasm, to come on strong, and so he stands up on the line, looks down at the prospect, and shouts (by his actions, if not by his words), "Come on up here. Trust me! I'll take care of you."

How does the prospect respond to this display of emotion? He senses that something's not quite right. And he begins moving toward 7, even farther away from the close.

How could this situation have been handled with greater success?

When the prospect was at 4, the professional salesperson would move to safer ground, say, 5 or 6, but surely not 3. It's a big mistake to get between your prospect's location on the clock and the point at which you want your prospect to arrive. Don't get in the way of the sale! If you do, you'll become the problem, as happened to the traditionally trained salesperson above. Frighten the prospect, and you're likely to kill the sale.

So when the 4 prospect says: "I really like your service," the wise salesperson responds: "That's fine. However, are you sure you've given this enough thought?" With that gentle negative reverse, the salesperson moves below the prospect. No pressure. No threat. Just reassurance and the beginning of establishing rapport.

PROSPECT *(perhaps moving away from 4 as he thinks about the salesperson's question):*
Well, I'm not sure about that.

SALESPERSON *(nurturingly, gently, and still behind the prospect's position on the clock):*
Maybe there is something else you would like to ask me before you decide to make this investment. For example, you could have asked me about . . .

The prospect has slipped back to 5, but he begins asking the salesperson some questions.

"Now wait a minute," you might protest, "the prospect is moving away from the close!"

You're right. And remember Newton's law: a body in motion stays in motion? The salesperson's patience and nurturing reverses moved the prospect, and it doesn't matter that the prospect moved farther away from 3. Now that the prospect is in motion, he'll stay in motion. However, by reversing, the sales pro will eventually lead (rather than drag) the prospect back to 3. It'll happen. And when the prospect arrives at 3, the deal is done, and the prospect thinks he got there all by himself! As long as the salesperson continues reversing the prospect, sooner or later, the prospect will swing up to 3 o'clock. It's the law!

Too Much Negative Reverse Selling Isn't Positive!

Not long after developing the Negative Reverse Selling technique, I had the opportunity to call on a local Ford agency. The sales manager invited me to speak to nine of his salespeople, but a couple of things went wrong.

First, the sales manager asked me to come in at eight o'clock in the morning, and I later found out that people who sell cars don't like to get to work until midmorning, at about ten o'clock.

Second, the manager introduced me to his group of salespeople, told them I had a sales training program they should look at, and then left the room. I shouldn't have let that happen.

I was excited about the Negative Reverse Selling technique, so I began by saying, "I am here to talk to you about a sales training program, and I think it's worthwhile. The sales manager thinks it's worthwhile too. But if there is anyone in the room who has no interest in listening to a sales training presentation, this is the time to leave."

Nine people got up and left the room!

It was embarrassing getting from the training room to the front door. That morning, I questioned whether or not Negative Reverse Selling would work. What I learned is that there's a limit to how much negative reversing you can do, and there's also a proper time to use it!

Consider, now, a prospect who's stuck at 6 o'clock, indifferent to the salesperson. How will the traditionalist handle this prospect? By dashing to the 3 o'clock and showing more excitement, of course. That's how she's been trained. But the more animated she becomes—it's called "being enthusiastic" in the traditional world—the more suspicious the prospect becomes. And very quickly the prospect moves from 7 to 8 to 9 o'clock . . . and there's no deal.

How would the professional salesperson handle this situation? With the prospect at 6, the salesperson moves to 9 o'clock. (That's "It's over"!) He's got to get the prospect into motion. A body at rest remains at rest! The pro knows better than to get in the way of the deal. He's got to work from a point that won't frighten or threaten the prospect. By perching himself at 9 o'clock and gently reversing the prospect, the salesperson builds rapport and gives the prospect space. The prospect feels secure, comfortable, and in control. And that's when he begins to move. True, the prospect is moving toward 9 o'clock, but it makes no difference at this point. The salesperson has Newton in his corner! A body in motion stays in motion.

The professional salesperson is only too happy to see the prospect swing all the way up to 9 o'clock. Remember, this is a pendulum. When the prospect reaches 9 o'clock, there's only one direction for him to go—back to where he came from. But instead of stopping at 6 o'clock, this prospect will swing all the way up to 3 o'clock, empowered by the nurturing forces of Negative Reverse Selling. Even more exciting, the prospect thinks he got to three o'clock all by himself!

Look what happens to the prospect who *starts* at 9 o'clock ("It's over!"). Traditionalists fear this prospect most of all. They can't budge someone who is negative. So what do they do? The only thing they know how to do. Hop up to the horizontal line, over at 3, and jump up and down, yell and shout, and try to get the prospect's attention. The negative prospect is so far away, however, that he can't even hear the salesperson. There's no motion in this scenario, and it will soon end unsuccessfully.

How does the professional salesperson respond to the negative prospect? He gets behind the prospect at 9 o'clock, or even 10 o'clock. And what's he doing? Talking more negatively than the prospect! Why? You've probably figured that out by now. If the salesperson can get the prospect to pull against his line, and he begins to swing toward 6 (neutral), the same law applies. Once the prospect begins to move, there's a good chance he'll swing all the way up to 3. The technique to get him there? Negative Reverse Selling!

A negative prospect requires the ultimate reverse, and it goes like this:

"Mr. Jones, based on what you have told me so far, my feeling is that you have absolutely no interest in what I am selling. So, before I leave, can I ask you one last question: *Is it over?*"

Watch what happens to the prospect now! Prospects don't want things to be over. They just want to be in control:

PROSPECT: *Well, I never said it was over.*

SALESPERSON *(Carefully now. Patiently.)*: *I guess I misunderstood you. What did you say?*

No matter what the prospect says now, the salesperson is back in the selling process again! The prospect has no idea what hit him; in fact, he thinks he's in control.

But what about the prospect who says, "Yes, it is over." It happens, but only rarely. In that event, the salesperson says: "Before I leave, now that it's over, can I ask you a question?" (That's Lieutenant Columbo talking, by the way: "Oh, one more thing . . .")

The prospect always says "yes" to this request. The next question—regardless of what it is—starts up the selling process once again, with a chance to get the prospect into motion.

Here's another way to approach the prospect who says it's over: "Now that it is over, can I stop being a salesperson for a minute and be a consultant?" Or if you don't like the word "salesperson," say: "Can I take off my technical hat for a moment and be a consultant?" This sets up an opportunity for the salesperson to say whatever is on his or her mind. There's no sense in holding back now. The prospect is at nine o'clock; if he can't be set in motion, it makes no difference what you say or do. So don't hold back! Your response just might get the prospect moving, and then you're back in the selling process.

How about the prospect who begins at 3 o'clock (sold)? A safe and easy close? That's what the traditionally trained salesperson thinks. But wait a minute. How did the prospect get to three o'clock so fast? By reading a brochure, seeing an ad, or talking to a friend? Maybe so, but before I explain how to handle this situation, try this:

Stick your arm out at the 3 o'clock. Notice how it got there? You had to swing it out or up, didn't you? How long can you hold it there? Depending on their physical condition, some people can hold it there longer than others. But eventually—remember what Newton said—the arm will have to come down. Things in motion stay in motion! Sooner or later the arm will fall; we just don't know when. That's precisely the danger of meeting with a prospect who's in the sold position. A prospect who's "too sold" too early is dangerous, unless the salesperson knows how to handle the situation. What should the professional salesperson do? Move to 6 o'clock and gently reverse the prospect into motion. After a couple of reverses, the prospect will no longer be "oversold." So the salesperson can let go. What happens? The prospect will swing back to 3, where the sale will be successfully closed.

To Get Rid of a Bomb, Defuse It Before It Blows!

If there's a recurring problem with your product or service, don't put yourself under stress wondering when your prospect is going to ask the question that sets off the bomb. Bring it up yourself, and defuse the bomb.

Here's an example:

SALESPERSON: *One of the problems we may have, Harry, assuming we decide to do business together, is that we don't provide local service. Is that going to be a problem?*

PROSPECT: *Yes.*

SALESPERSON: *You start.*

Bringing up the problem makes it easier for you to handle the potential objections rather than waiting to face the problem defensively.

By now you should understand why Negative Reverse Selling is one of the most powerful techniques in the arsenal of the Sandler Selling System. However, it wouldn't surprise me if you were feeling uncertain about it because it's the most difficult technique to "own." For one thing, if you've been trained traditionally, it's a reverse of what you've already been taught to do.

Furthermore, Negative Reverse Selling demands that you behave differently. How so? Well, when you use this technique, you will become a gentler, kinder salesperson. There's no longer any risk of looking like the old backslapping, plaid-jacket-clad salesperson whom everyone fears. Negative Reverse Selling allows you to be calm and relaxed. It removes the pressure from the sales call. The prospect responds favorably to your patience and nurturing attitude. It's a powerful technique that works, and makes money, if you'll give it a chance.

To use it, however, you've got to own it, and to own it requires practice. I encourage you to try it. Don't rush it. Keep your line in the water, and use a little bit of fishing sense!

On the other hand, maybe Negative Reverse Selling is too extreme for your style? In fact, maybe you shouldn't try it all. Perhaps you should just forget that you ever heard about Negative Reverse Selling. But let me ask you this: Is it over?

9

"GOOD MORNING, SIR, IS THAT YOUR SAILFISH?"

The way people get to feel OK about

themselves is to find someone who

is more Not-OK than they are.

—DAVID H. SANDLER

There are two versions of successful Bonding and Rapport. There's the short version, which I'm going to tell you in a moment, and the long version, which fills out the balance of this chapter (which you may elect not to read).

Here's the short version:

Always make the prospect (or customer) feel more OK than you feel. That's it. End of story. Do it and you'll succeed!

You really don't have to read the rest of this chapter. I suggest you review the I/R Theory in Chapter 3. Then, practice the advice above, and you'll do just fine at Bonding and Rapport. In fact, you're off to a great start as a professional salesperson.

The first compartment of the Sandler Submarine has been closed!

But wait a minute. What would happen if I ended the chapter now? The short version *really does* say it all about Bonding and Rapport. And some of you—those who understand that Bonding and Rapport is simply the act of always making your prospect (or customer) feel good—no doubt agree with me. So what's the sense of sharing the long version? Why not just move forward to the next compartment of the Sandler Submarine?

> Always make the prospect (or customer) feel more OK than you feel.

My internal editor tells me that without sharing the long version, I would violate the most important rule of human relations, which says: *The way people get to feel OK about themselves is to find someone who is more Not-OK than they are.* The short version might be sufficient for some people, but it's likely to leave many people feeling Not-OK for any number of reasons. Consequently, if I don't share the long version, I'll lose those readers. There will be no opportunity to win them over to my ideas because there was never any bonding, never any rapport. I made them feel worse, not better. I gave them a reason *not* to buy anything I have to offer.

Making people feel Not-OK about themselves is the fastest way to end a relationship, or sink the sale. So allow me to share the long version to successful Bonding and Rapport. That way, I've got the chance to satisfy everyone. To begin the long version, let's return to the most important rule of human relations, which says: *The way people get to feel OK about themselves is to find someone who is more Not-OK than they are.*

As harsh as that sounds, it's true. I learned that lesson as a child watching Tarzan movies. When I was a kid, my mom used to give me 15 cents to go with my friends to the corner movie to see Tarzan every Saturday afternoon. A bunch of us kids occupied the front row of the theater. The screen was so big that we could hardly see it all, but that didn't matter.

I remember it this way: As the picture opens, there's Tarzan, sitting in his hut, and there's little Cheetah with a bunch of bananas. Suddenly, the screen changes, and there's a man walking throughout the jungle wearing a safari helmet and carrying a backpack. He's big. Seems like seven feet tall. And he's chopping his way through the jungle when all of a sudden he steps into quicksand.

The screen changes again, and now the man is sinking and he's scrambling to get to solid ground, but he can't get loose. He's going down, and he starts yelling: "Help, help, help, oh someone, help me!"

Next scene: Tarzan hears the screams. He jumps up from his hut, grabs the closest vine, and begins flying through the jungle from vine to vine, flying ever closer to the man in trouble. By the time Tarzan reaches the ground, Cheetah, Boy, Jane, and even the elephant are all behind him. Wow, this is exciting!

What do you think a bunch of six-year-old kids in the first row are doing at this point of the movie? Are we yelling, "Go, Tarzan, go!"?

Absolutely not!

I always wanted the guy to sink, and so did my friends. Why? If you don't know, let me tell you something. Life was tough for a six-year-old kid. But for one moment, we were more OK than that guy on the screen. And it made us feel better to see him in trouble. Not only him, but anyone else who was more Not-OK than we were. We loved it when the Road Runner knocked the Coyote off the cliff, or when Bugs Bunny whacked Elmer Fudd over the head!

Today, I'd have an entirely different reaction to these childhood pastimes, but kids aren't the only people who feel better at someone else's expense. Adults look for those opportunities all the time. How else can we explain the success of soap operas? These popular TV series are faithfully followed by millions of people daily. Most soap opera plots are unrealistic and loaded with misfortune, but men and women follow these dramas and bond with certain characters if for no other reason than the chance to feel better about themselves.

Amateur Salespeople Are for the Birds

Amateur salespeople make professional salespeople look bad. They tend to be overenthusiastic, impatient, too animated, and downright insulting.

Amateur salespeople look like vultures sitting on a telephone wire, waiting for a squirrel to get hit by a car.

The professional salesperson, on the other hand, is always in control, patiently waits for "the kill," and is a credit to our profession.

As you critique your future sales calls, review your selling techniques, but also think about how you appeared in front of the prospect. Relax. Don't come "off the wire" too quickly, and you'll go to the bank more often!

What's this got to do with your life as a professional salesperson? Easy. Use this rule of human relations to your advantage. Make yourself Not-OK *on purpose,* and you'll automatically make your prospect (or customer) feel OK. By being Not-OK in front of a prospect, you strip away all the preconceived notions the prospect has inherited about your profession, the buyer-seller dance, and you as a salesperson. You're not a threat when you act Not-OK.

Am I telling you not to be professional? Am I telling you to act stupid? No, on both accounts. By acting Not-OK, I mean that you should not flex your intellectual muscle. Don't act superior. Don't use buzz-words. Don't appear to be Mr. or Ms. All-Together.

Struggle a little bit!

At first, it'll be difficult—or awkward—struggling on purpose. But every technique created by Sandler Training requires practice—rein-forcement training—to accomplish it.

Let me tell you another personal story. One of my first jobs was buying national advertising for a company. I didn't know much about this subject, so I did my best to educate myself. One afternoon an experienced salesperson came to visit me with the plan to sell me some advertising. I immediately thought to myself, "This guy knows his stuff. I can learn from this guy." I was, in fact, bonding with this salesperson, and I planned to buy from him until he said to me, "By the way, have you ever had spots before?"

Suddenly, I didn't know what he meant. He couldn't be talking about measles. And yet, up to that point, it was only a case of measles that had given me spots. Since I didn't know what he meant, I started feeling Not-OK. And since I didn't want to look stupid, I said to him, "Excuse me. I have another appointment. You'll have to get back to me in a few days." And that was the end of the sales call.

What happened? The OK/Not-OK Rule went into effect without my even knowing it existed. It's a normal reaction. When someone makes you feel Not-OK, you will fight for OK-ness by getting rid of the one who makes you feel Not- OK. One super salesperson who used a buzz-word lost his opportunity to make a sale. It was safer for me to get rid of him than to admit that I didn't know if I had ever had "spots" before.

How much wiser it would have been for him to struggle a little bit!

How do you struggle *on purpose?* Here are several rules to follow:

1. Use dummy-up phrases like "I don't understand" or "Can you help me with that?" or "What do you mean, exactly?"
2. Even if you have every answer at your fingertips, look like you don't.
3. Never use buzzwords.
4. Be assertive, not aggressive.
5. Allow your prospects to "know it all" and get their OK-ness needs met. Avoid playing one-upmanship.

6. Appear to be lost in a prospect's office. Go left when you know the way out is right.

Fake It Till You Make It

Sales are often lost when the prospect senses the salesperson *needs* the order. A salesperson can telegraph such a message through nervous reactions, body language, hesitancy, and so forth.

In fact, there will be times when you really do need the order! An effective technique to help you stay in control during these times is to repeat to yourself over and over again: "I am financially independent, and I don't need the business."

If that were the truth, wouldn't you then know what to say? You'll find that when you're convinced you don't need the business, you'll use the Sandler techniques professionally and with ease.

When you learn how to struggle, you will immediately begin to make your prospects and customers feel better about themselves. Take that away from them, and what's left? The revolving door. Make someone feel Not-OK, and you're history. Help them feel OK, and you'll become a *part* of their history.

Who taught us that lesson better than former president Ronald Reagan, who enjoyed two terms in the White House? Whether you supported him or not, no one would disagree that Reagan was a master at articulating the simple truths that defined the meaning of America. It was Reagan's ability to speak to the American people that led to him being dubbed "the Great Communicator."

Reagan made communicating seem easy because he worked so hard at it. And even so, he struggled. He understood that communication is a two-way street. He read the public's mood and responded accordingly. His speeches were in a language that his audiences could appreciate— simple and dramatic—and they were brought to life by stories from the real world. Reagan made people feel OK. In the process, he sold himself and became a part of American history.

As a salesperson, the most important skill to learn is the ability to communicate. It's the basis for establishing Bonding and Rapport.

SANDLER SELLING TIP

People buy emotionally, and they justify their decisions intellectually. Prospects are not as interested in the features and benefits as they are in finding a way to remove the pain they presently have. They are also concerned with finding a way to *avoid* pain they anticipate having in the future. These are emotional impulses! The intellect comes into play only when people want to justify a purchase. Here's the challenge though. If you don't establish Bonding and Rapport throughout the sales discussion, and if you do not ensure that the prospect *always* feels OK enough to share his or her emotions with you, there's no driving reason to buy!

This leads us to one of the perils of attempting to conduct a discussion with a prospect without the benefit of verbal or body language cues—via a series of email exchanges, say, that never turn into a real-time, one-on-one conversation. In these situations, you have no idea whether or not you've actually established Bonding and Rapport! No matter how compelling the logic of the case you make via email, you will have a hard time figuring out whether you have tapped into the emotional currents that actually drive a sale.

—DHM

What Is Rapport?

The French originated the word *rapport* to mean "to bring back or offer back." However, the French use the word most often in the phrase *en rapport avec*, meaning "to be in connection with someone."

Simply said, rapport is sharing a common point of view. By mastering rapport skills, you will bond more quickly with your prospects and influence them to become your customers and clients.

When you walk into a prospect's office, what do you do now to establish rapport? Traditionally, salespeople look for something in the office that raises a question. For example, "Is that your sailfish on the wall?"

How many times do you think that prospect has been asked that question? How often do you think the prospect hears a salesperson ask about the family portrait on the wall, the golf clubs in the corner, or the collection of clowns on the bookshelf? I won't disagree that these questions help to establish rapport, but the prospect *anticipates* them. They're amateurish and outdated.

In face-to-face communications, the words we speak often express the smallest amount of the message—perhaps as little as 10 percent—especially when conveying thoughts, concepts, feelings, or abstract elements. The tonality of our speech—rate, pitch, and volume—communicate quite a bit more information, approximately 35 to 40 percent. Body language—facial expressions and gestures—make up the balance, 50 percent or more.

To communicate effectively and to ensure that the listener gets the meaning you intended, your tonality and body language must be consistent with the words you speak. If, for instance, there is hesitancy in your voice or a look of uncertainty on your face, the listener will likely doubt the accuracy or sincerity of your words.

In a similar manner, you must be aware of your prospects' tonality and body language and their consistency (or lack of consistency) with the words they speak. If you sense any discrepancies, acknowledge and deal with them immediately.

Physiology: Nonverbal Communication

As we have seen, a great deal of rapport is established through nonverbal communication.

To many people, this suggests the need to learn to read body language. For example, if you're sitting across from your prospect, Lila, and she has her arms folded, body language experts might tell you that means she's "closed" to whatever it is you're saying.

But it's not that simple. Maybe Lila's closed, or maybe she's most comfortable with her arms folded. Doesn't matter. It's much more important to delve into Lila's physical patterns and mirror those patterns. How does she move? How does she sit? Look and see, and then do the same thing. Don't try to guess what a particular body movement means. Just mirror it!

People feel most comfortable with themselves. As a professional salesperson, you need to match your prospects' body language so that the prospects feel comfortable with you as a reflection of them. People feel comfortable with other people who are like themselves!

As you match and mirror your prospect's physiology, you don't have to worry about looking like an exact image of the prospect. That's not important. Physiology works at the subconscious level. The prospect isn't going to say, "This salesperson looks just like me. Therefore, I like him." Instead, the message forms subconsciously, and as it reaches the prospect, the prospect relaxes and feels comfortable in your presence. Now you have rapport!

Tonality: How You Sound Is Important

While people feel comfortable with other people who are like themselves, it's also true that people feel comfortable with other people who *sound* like themselves.

When you listen to someone speak, concentrate on the several subsets of tonality, which are volume, rate of speech, tone, tempo, and favorite words and phrases.

Have you been on a sales call where you spoke loudly and your prospect spoke in a much lower voice, or vice versa? It doesn't seem like something so trivial would matter, but it does. Put yourself in the prospect's place. You generally speak in a very loud voice, and the salesperson across from you uses a very soft voice. Does that make you feel comfortable or uncomfortable? OK or Not-OK?

What's your rate of speech? Is it fast, slow, or in between? When you're with a prospect, do you speak at your own rate, or do you mirror the prospect's rate of speech? Put yourself in the prospect's place once again. You speak slowly. You like to pick and choose your words carefully. You like to leave a little thinking time between your sentences. But

> People feel comfortable with other people who are like themselves!

there's this salesperson across from you, and he's speaking so fast that you can't even think. How do you feel? What are you thinking? Are you likely to say to yourself, "I like this guy. He talks fast." Or might you say to yourself, "This guy is slick. I'm not sure I can trust him."

Maybe when you were a youngster, your mother or father said to you, "It's not what you said. It's your tone of voice that I don't like!" Well, prospects can react the same way to a salesperson's tone of voice. A squeaky, high-pitched tone is irritating to all but the people who use the same tone. Equally bad is a tone that's sarcastic, all-knowing, or gruff. The tone that's most pleasing to your prospect is the tone you hear your prospect using.

Tempo, or the rhythm of conversation, is important too. Some people begin speaking slowly, and they build up speed as they become more emotional in their conversation. Others begin speaking emotionally and then wind down to a monotone, as though they've burned out before finishing. Pay attention to tempo, and begin to mirror the tempo that you hear in conversations with your prospects.

Listen for your prospect's favorite words and phrases, and then "play them back" for your prospect. Words and phrases have special meaning to people. Listen for them, write them in your notes, and use them later in your conversation and in future meetings with your prospect or customer. By using favorite words and phrases, you demonstrate that you are in rapport with your prospect's belief system.

Tonality definitely affects rapport, so it's important to understand and practice the various subsets of tonality.

Verbal: Show, Tell, and Touch

Many traditional salespeople spend thousands of dollars annually to hone their speaking skills because they think this will help them establish rapport faster and easier with their prospects and customers. And yet, we know that verbal skill is a comparatively small piece of the rapport quotient. Walking into a room and talking about who won last night's baseball game, or what the weather is about to do, might begin to set the stage for rapport with some prospects, but for most prospects, it's meaningless gibberish.

Why so? All of us interpret our personal environment through our senses, which act like filters. Thousands of things happen to us in any given day, and our minds have to make sense of everything. Your mind is constantly asking: "How does what just happened fit into my world? How do I make sense of that?" Your mind asks those questions constantly as untold numbers of stimuli enter your brain. How do you categorize the answers and fit everything into your world?

You use your senses: sight, smell, sound, touch, and taste. For certain stimuli you use only one of these senses; for others, you use some combination of the senses.

In the business world, three senses are dominant: sight, sound, and touch. (Unless you sell a food product, you generally cannot give your prospect the opportunity to taste or smell.)

Most of the time, your prospects rely on one sense more than the others to make decisions. Prospects are either *visual* people, meaning they need to see a picture before they can make a decision; or they are *auditory,* meaning they need to hear something before they can make a decision; or they are *kinesthetic,* meaning they need to touch or feel something to make a decision. Some combination of these senses is at work in all prospects, but one sense dominates.

So look what happens when your prospect is kinesthetic and you walk into the room and say: "How about those Cowboys. Did you see the game yesterday?" You're trying to establish rapport, but how does your *kinesthetic* prospect—who needs to touch—gain any sense of commonality out of what you said?

If your research told you the prospect is a Cowboys fan, and you also learned that the prospect is kinesthetic, you'd want to say: "Wow, doesn't it make you *feel* great when those Cowboys win?" Your kinesthetic prospect knows, indeed, what it *feels* like when the Cowboys win or lose.

Before you can begin to establish rapport with a prospect or bond with a customer, you need to determine if you're talking to a visual, auditory, or kinesthetic person.

Once you figure that out, it's like someone handing you an instruction manual to the prospect! Rapport is almost instantaneous when you speak the prospect's language and enter the prospect's world.

How can you tell which sense dominates the prospect's decision-making engine? Listen for the clues. Every prospect will give them to you. Just listen to what the prospect says.

A visual prospect will say something like this: "That seems a little *fuzzy* to me. Can you *show* me a picture? I'm having some trouble *focusing* on that idea. I'd like to *see* that in my *mind's eye.*" Visual people use their eyes to view the world around them, and they need visual images to communicate. If you want to sell a visual prospect, you've got to speak visually. "What do you see yourself accomplishing?" is a good question to ask a visual prospect.

An auditory prospect will say something like this: "What does it sound like when you make the connection? Can you *comment on* the importance of this gadget? I've got to make it *clear as a bell* in order to *announce* it at the next level." Auditory people use their ears to make sense of the world. Next time you go to a concert, look around for the people who have their eyes closed. They're not sleeping; they're listening. They don't need to see the orchestra to enjoy the music.

A kinesthetic prospect will say something like this: "It *feels* a little *muddled* to me. It's got to fit *hand in hand* with what we're already doing. It's a *sensitive* issue, and I've got to be *comfortable* with it." The kinesthetic prospect seeks trust. Learn to create the feeling of trust, and you can quickly establish rapport with a kinesthetic person. Equally important: kinesthetics want to know that you *care* about them.

By "reading" your prospects' clues and "living" in their world, you can quickly establish rapport and begin to improve your sales proficiency. Your goal as a salesperson is to learn these Bonding and Rapport techniques, practice them repeatedly, and adapt them to your business and social lives. When you do, your quality of life will dramatically improve. (Sandler franchisees provide weekly practice sessions for professional salespeople to meet and hone their skills. Visit us at www.sandler.com for more information about a meeting in your area.)

The bottom line of professional selling, as viewed by Sandler Training, is going to the bank. It's not about getting your OK-ness needs met. Want to go to the bank more often? The shortest way there is to *always make the prospect (or customer) feel more OK than you feel.* Which brings us right back to where we began!

10

DON'T DO ANYTHING UNLESS YOU KNOW WHY YOU'RE DOING IT!

The most important Up-Front Contract you will ever make is with yourself. It's the contract that says nothing will drive you out of sales.

—DAVID H. SANDLER

The most assertive step in the Sandler Selling System is the Up-Front Contract, and it's all to your advantage!

Up-Front Contracting throws prospects off balance. They don't expect it. They never see it coming. It's painless, honest, and effective, and when it's handled correctly, the sale has been closed. You know it, but the prospect doesn't find out until later. As I said, it's all to your advantage!

I originally created the Up-Front Contract for my own defense. In the early days of my career, the thing that scared me the most, as you already know, was cold calling. I was afraid to show up at a prospect's office to try to make a sale. I knew the routine well enough—too well, in fact. Get in the door, establish some rapport, do the dog-and-pony show, handle the stalls and objections, close, then fight, fight, fight!

Three "Noes" to Avoid When Setting Up-Front Contracts

1. **No mutual mystification.** Any communication you have with your prospect must have a clear understanding about what happens next.
2. **No wishy-washy words.** When a prospect says to you "Things look good, Sue, and I'm hoping that next week we might be able to do something," you might think, "Wow! I've got the order." But the prospect is thinking, "I'm not sure who I'll give this order to." Chances are it might not be you! Better to clarify the wishy-washy words.
3. **No smoke.** Your "gut" is your built-in smoke detector. Learn to rely on it. When you establish an Up-Front Contract, that means there's

no guessing, no surprises, no assumptions. It doesn't guarantee the sales, but it makes selling less stressful and more enjoyable.

But what if I didn't know all the answers to questions about my product? And what if I gave a terrific presentation, but at the end of it the prospect said, "No!"? I didn't want to fail. I wanted to succeed! Too often I would sit in front of a prospect's office and just stare at the door, thinking negatively. Other times, I would drive around the block for an hour pretending my car door was welded shut. Hard to believe, but it even made me happy if the line was busy when I placed a sales call by phone. I just didn't want to start the process!

One day the thought occurred to me to break down the selling process into compartments. All I really needed to do was establish an agreement with the prospect to see if we had anything to discuss, and if so, we could continue to determine if we should do business together. If there was nothing to discuss, no harm done. That was easy! This meant I could call on anyone and never risk failing. I couldn't fail trying to make a contract. Either I got a contract or I didn't. If I did, all the better; and if I didn't, I was out the door, no regrets. Suddenly, selling became more of a game than a risk or a challenge.

Use the Up-Front Contract to Set an Agenda

As soon as you get in front of a prospect, and you've completed the Bonding and Rapport compartment of the Sandler Submarine, set the agenda for the sales call. Here are several approaches you can use:

> "Bill, what are some of the things you'd like to accomplish today?"

> "Linda, when we were on the telephone, I asked you to write down five of the major problems you're having with [blank]. Can you share some of them with me?"

> "Mary, I've been in sales for several years, and I have numerous clients. I've found there are no accidents. I believe there's a

reason why we're getting together today. What motivated you to invite me in?"

"Kevin, last week when we spoke on the phone and you invited me in, what were you hoping I could do for you?"

If your prospect has invited you in as a result of an advertisement or an article in a magazine or a direct-mail piece, use this approach:

"Jim, what was it about the brochure [or letter, advertisement, mail piece, or something else] that caught your attention? Why did you invite me in?"

Take notes when your prospects respond. It's a way to show you care about their problems.

If you think of selling as a game, then why shouldn't you use Up-Front Contracts? Every other sport does. Before a baseball game, the umpire calls the managers from the opposing teams to home plate, and they discuss the rules of baseball. They agree on what's foul and fair and what makes a home run, and they review any unusual circumstances about the ballpark. So later, during the game, if a batter hits a ball behind the catcher, up over the screen, and into the crowd, there's no argument that it's a foul ball. And when the batter hits the ball over the fence between the left and right outfield foul posts, there's no argument that it's a home run. Imagine the confusion, however, had the managers and the umpire not agreed, up front, about the rules of the game.

Why don't salespeople take the same approach? What could be more honest than to establish a set of rules at the beginning of interacting with a prospect? An Up-Front Contract, or better yet, a series of Up-Front Contracts, will save time for both you and the prospect, and it will help you make more money in sales without offending anyone. By always arriving at an agreement up front, you and the prospect can avoid misunderstandings, as well as the rhetoric and posturing that often occur during the selling dance. An Up-Front Contract improves communications and greatly enhances the profession of selling. I urge you to begin using this technique today!

Control Your Fears with the Up-Front Contract

What scares you about the selling process? Which part of the selling process causes you the most stress? Whatever it is (and maybe it's nothing at all), deal with it by using the Up-Front Contract.

Let's assume you stumble over asking for money in the selling process. Here's how you can solve the problem:

"Chuck, before I begin talking to you about my product [or service], let me tell you about my biggest concern. I'm afraid that when I get to the end of the presentation, you're going to like what you see and hear, but I'm going to have difficulty asking you for money. That's always been something that gets in my way. I have trouble asking for money. So to get that out of the way, and to ease my mind so I can give you my best presentation, are you OK dealing with money up front?"

Using this approach, you substitute any problem or word for "money" and get your prospect to agree to discuss it first.

The Up-Front Contract is an amazing sales tool, don't you agree?

An Up-Front Contract is based on the legal concept of a contract. Any valid legal contract consists of four major components and several minor components. On paper, here's what it looks like:

1. Lawful object
2. Competency
3. Consideration
4. Mutual consent
   A. Understanding
   B. A proposal, verbal or written
   C. Acceptance

First, you can't have an Up-Front Contract if you don't have a *lawful object*, that is, a product or service to sell. And it's got to be legal.

Second, an Up-Front Contract requires *competency* between the salesperson and the prospect. You must have the authority to make an offer, as well as close the sale, and the prospect must have the authority to accept it. You can give the greatest presentation in the world, but if you can't deliver, or if the prospect can't accept your offer, what's the use? No contract can follow.

Third, an Up-Front Contract requires some form of *consideration*. For all practical purposes, let's assume it's money.

Finally, a valid Up-Front Contract includes *mutual consent,* which means that you *offer* to do something such as make a presentation, come back for a follow-up visit, or solve a problem, and the prospect *accepts* your offer. Notice that I did not say you offered to sell your product or service and the prospect agreed to buy it. That *could be* the offer, but it's not likely to be this early in the game. However, if you master Up-Front Contracting, you'll seldom have to offer your product or service for the sale. After fulfilling a series of Up-Front Contracts, prospects close themselves!

SANDLER SELLING TIP

An Up-Front Contract with a prospect must contain the following five elements:

1. **Objective.** (This is our starting goal, a goal the prospect shares with us.)
2. **Time allotted.** (If the meeting will take an hour, the prospect should agree with us that an hour will be set aside.)
3. **Our role to get us there.** (This is what we'll be doing before, during, and after the discussion.)
4. **Prospect's role to get us there.** (This is what the prospect will be doing before, during, and after the discussion.)
5. **Conclusion.** (This is a preview of the forthcoming discussion's possible end position; there may well be more than one possible conclusion, but the prospect must agree with us on what they all are.)

We train salespeople to use Microsoft Outlook's "meeting invite" function to restate and solidify the five elements of the Up-Front Contract that the salesperson and the prospect have agreed to verbally.   —DHM

The Up-Front Contract Works by Telephone Too

If you use the telephone to set up appointments or to sell, here are some useful tips:

1. **Get the appointment.** Convince the prospect to invite you in for a sales meeting. Say something like this: "George, let me tell you what I think makes sense. Why don't you invite me over, and we'll find out if there is anything that I have that can help you. Does that make sense to you?"

2. **Confirm the appointment.** "Before we hang up, is there any chance you might have to change this appointment?" If the prospect says yes, you say: "Could we do that now? I run a rather tight schedule, and I'm sure you do too." Fight for a firm appointment. If the prospect says no to the question about the chance of changing the appointment, you say: "The only reason I brought that up is that sometimes, and it's probably not the case here, people tend to set appointments casually. Like me, I'm sure you appreciate the value of using time well. Sorry I brought it up, but you know how most people are. See you [repeat the date of the appointment]."

3. **Assign homework prior to the next call.** "So that we can make our next call productive, here's what we need to do. When I call back, let's go over any questions you may have. We'll spend as much time as you need to get comfortable. At the end of the call, let's decide either to move forward or to close your file. That way neither one of us will get hung up in a game of telephone tag. Does that make sense to you?"

4. **Don't accept "I'll think it over" for a response.** "What we don't want to happen is for us to get into a drawn-out 'think it over' scenario where we both become frustrated and worn out. Is that OK? Do you have any questions before I hang up?"

5. **Qualify the prospect during your conversation.** "Since we're going to do most of our work by phone, Jim, it would help me if you could let me in on what your decision-making process generally looks like. OK?"

In the early stages of the sales call, the offer itself is less important than what I'm going to say next: *the offer must be explicitly communicated and certain in its terms.* In other words, there can be no doubt about what you offered the prospect.

Too often, the interaction between salesperson and prospect is fuzzy. Neither side really understands what transpired between them. Ever hear a prospect say, "Well, George, certainly based on what you're telling me so far, all things being equal, apples for apples, it really looks good. You're very close. I don't see any reason in the long run why you may not get this order, assuming things fall into shape and everything works out well."

On that note, the amateur salesperson rushes back to the office and says, "Boss, got one!" when, in fact, he has nothing at all. The more intelligent salesperson would recognize the prospect's wishy-washy response. And using the Sandler Selling System, you would not accept such verbiage from a prospect.

To make an intelligent offer, you must first *understand* the prospect's problem, or what I call "pain." As I'll soon explain, this process requires you to ask a variety of questions and to listen while the prospect does most of the talking. There should be no doubt in your mind about the prospect's needs. If there is, you've got to ask clarifying questions to clear out the smoke.

The message that you want to send to your prospect as quickly as possible in your first meeting is that you really *understand* the problem from the prospect's point of view. In a survey conducted some years ago by *Harvard Business Review*, business owners said their major fear while hiring outside consultants was that the consultant would not understand their business.

Here's how you can demonstrate to prospects that you want to understand their problem, or business, and at the same time establish an Up-Front Contract. Look how this statement sets the ground rules for the meeting between salesperson and prospect:

"Liz, I'd like to ask you some questions to make sure I can understand your business and to make sure I understand your concerns. You probably want to ask me some questions to see if we're the right kind of company for you.

"As we ask and answer each other's questions, two things can happen. You might say, 'Your answers don't help my problem,' and if that happens, so that we don't waste each other's time, are you OK telling me no? You can say, 'Hey, Steve, stop. I don't think there's anything we can do together.'

"On the other hand, Liz, it's possible that we might see eye to eye on what we are discussing, and in that case, I would expect you to say 'Yes.' What I hope you won't say is, 'I want to think it over.' If you feel like you have to think it over, I'd rather you say 'No.' Are you OK telling me that, Liz?"

When Liz *accepts* the offer, that's an Up-Front Contract. See how it works? Liz didn't agree to buy your service—and that's not what you offered—but she did agree to play the game with you by the ground rules that you established. The agreement includes a desire to understand the business, an offer to accept yes or no for an answer, and acceptance by Liz. There's no doubt about your mutual consent. But wait a minute. Have you forgotten that prospects are perfectly OK with misleading you? Never forget this! Your prospects probably aren't used to living up to verbal contracts with a salesperson. Prospects understand that they've got to pay the mortgage, the auto lease, and the credit card company, but they've never been trained to keep verbal commitments with salespeople.

Consequently, you've got to take your time with each Up-Front Contract and *validate* it. You can do that by going back over it or reviewing the statement:

"Liz, are you sure you're OK telling me no? Or if I can fill your needs, are you OK with telling me yes? It's not unusual for me to talk to people who say they're sure they're OK with this, but when it comes time to say no, most people don't like to do it. So I just want to be sure—do we have an understanding on this?"

Again, if Liz *accepts*, you've got a valid Up-Front Contract. Once she accepts, there's mutual consent.

Give Your Prospect the Opportunity to Say "Yes!"

If you set an Up-Front Contract that gives your prospect the opportunity to tell you no, be sure to also give the prospect the opportunity to say "Yes."

Here's how to do that:

"All right, Robyn, you know that a no is acceptable to me. You tell me no, and it's over. I'm out of your way. But let's suppose my answers fit what you're looking for. What happens then?"

Your prospects will believe they're in control if you give them the opportunity to tell you what happens next!

After establishing the ground rules by using an Up-Front Contract, it's easy to continue through the compartments of the Sandler Submarine using this powerful technique. At numerous points along the way, as you discuss pain, money, and decision, you will need to interject additional offers, creating a series of Up-Front Contracts. For example:

"Let me see if I understand what you're saying, Jerry. We've both agreed to A, B, and C, and you're comfortable with that, right? And the next step is for me to come in and show you A, B, and C, and if those items meet the criteria you've specified, then we go to the next step, which is to meet with your executive committee. Is that a fair assessment of where we are? And you're comfortable moving at this pace?"

If Jerry agrees, you've got an Up-Front Contract.

SANDLER SELLING TIP

Both sides need to know what is happening next and why.
Up-Front Contracts aren't just for one-on-one discussions with prospects. They're invaluable tools for clarifying discussion agendas, intentions, commitments, roles, and next steps with committees and work teams—and between sales manager and salesperson. —DHM

In a way, selling with the Up-Front Contract is like playing chess. You make a move, the prospect makes a move, then you move, the prospect moves, and so on. If one of you fails to make the proper move or makes no move at all, the game is over. For these reasons, it's important to establish an Up-Front Contract with your prospect prior to each move.

Always verify that your prospect understands the contract. Look at how easy it is to clarify your position with a prospect while also getting the prospect to state the contract:

"I believe I have a clear understanding of what we're trying to accomplish, Ron, but just so there's no misunderstanding at a later date, would you mind telling me what happened between us today so I can make sure we're in sync?"

If you don't hear what you thought happened, fix it before you make the next move . . . and shorten the selling cycle!

SANDLER SELLING TIP

Send stuff only after you establish an Up-Front Contract. Sooner or later, a prospect is going to say to you: "Email me something." It's a natural response to a salesperson. It's an easy way to reject the salesperson without getting personal.

Before you agree to send literature, ask yourself: "Why is the prospect requesting literature? Is this a sign of no interest?"

Ask the prospect:

"Maggie, it's no problem. I can email you some literature. But before I do, I need to ask you a question. OK?" (Notice the mini-Up-Front Contract? You've made an offer to do something—send literature—but you need to understand the situation better and thus you want to ask a question. And you're asking for the prospect's acceptance.)

Maggie agrees to let you ask a question, so you continue: "Sometimes when people ask me to email literature before they know anything about my product, as opposed to inviting me in, what they're really saying to me is they just don't have any interest. But they're too nice to tell me because they don't want to hurt my feelings. Is that the case here, Maggie?"

If you decide to send literature to a prospect, don't do it without an Up-Front Contract that explains what happens next.

"George, I have a tremendous amount of literature that may or may not be of interest to you. Do you mind if I ask you a few questions to make sure you'll be reviewing the right material before I email it?"

The questions you ask will do one of two things:

1. Narrow down the literature you need to send the prospect

2. Stir up enough interest in the prospect's mind to give you the opportunity to try a second time to set an appointment

If you've got to send literature, then continue as follows:

"I'm planning to email you the literature tomorrow, George. It's on its way. It should arrive by Thursday. How much time will you need to review it?"

Wait for George to respond and then say:

"You say you'll need 24 hours to review it, so I'll call you Friday. And here's what I'd like to have happen, if you're comfortable with this. I'd like you to be able to say, 'John, I read the literature, and I have some questions.' Or you can say, 'I've read the literature, and there's absolutely no reason for us to get together.' If you tell me you have some interest, George, then I'd like you to invite me in for a face-to-face meeting. Is that fair?" Set an Up-Front Contract before you email your literature. —DHM

The more often I used Up-Front Contracting in sales calls, the clearer it became to me that there was rarely a need to make a presentation. If you make a sales call, uncover the pain, discuss money, and make a decision, very often there's no need for the Fulfillment step of the system. Why? Because when you create a series of contracts, prospects can experience how your product or service will fulfill their needs. As you develop the contracts, you gently guide the prospects to see that your product or service can eliminate the problem or provide the solution.

By establishing Up-Front Contracts, you're not guaranteed to get every order, nor will you necessarily get an order today. However, establishing Up-Front Contracts will guarantee your control of the selling process, every step of the way.

As a salesperson, get in the habit of never making a move without knowing in advance what will happen when you do. Even small items require an Up-Front Contract. Say, for example, your prospect asks you to call back on Thursday, but you don't know why. Gently say, "Sally, I'll be happy to call you on Thursday. But let me ask you a question. What will happen when we talk on Thursday?" Note that softening statement "But let me ask you a question" removes the harshness from this technique.

Six Reasons to Use a Strong Up-Front Contract

1. It gives both the prospect and the salesperson the opportunity to ask questions.

   "Mr. Prospect, let's set some ground rules for our meeting. I'd like to have the opportunity to ask you some questions about your business, and I'd also like you to ask me anything you'd like about my product [or service]."

2. It gives both the prospect and the salesperson the opportunity to say "No" if there isn't a fit.

   "As we ask and answer each other's questions, Ms. Prospect, we may decide there isn't a fit between what you need and my service [or product]. We may decide it doesn't make sense to spend any more time together. If we reach that point, are you comfortable telling me that?"

3. It gives the prospect the opportunity to say "Yes" if there is a fit.

   "On the other hand, if you see that my service [or product] makes sense to you, we can decide to move forward. OK?"

4. It provides an end result for every sales call.

   "When we finish today, Ms. Prospect, we can set up the ground rules as to how you and I will proceed. Is that satisfactory?"

5. It allows for sufficient time during the sales call.

   "Bill, how much time have you set aside for this meeting? Your time is valuable, and so is mine, and I want to make sure not a minute gets wasted."

6. It establishes an agenda for the meeting.

   "Susan, what are some of the things you would like to accomplish today?" Or, "Bruce, I've been in this profession for a long time, and I have a lot of clients. I've found that there are no accidents. I believe there is a reason for our getting together. What motivated you to invite me in?"

If you want to improve your closing ratios, all you've got to do is become proficient at establishing strong Up-Front Contracts. It sounds simple, but it's asking a lot. It takes guts to make an Up-Front Contract. And it will probably require you to change your behavior. For decades, traditional sales trainers have taught us to sell their way, that is, the same old way. The prospect is in control, the salesperson is subservient, and it's anyone's guess who's going to win the tug-of-war. Traditions can't be dispelled all that easily. But try!

Practice Up-Front Contracting at home. Then, go out and do it. At first, it's going to feel awkward. You're going to get stumped. But remember, it's OK to fail. The more you use the technique, the faster you'll master it. I'd rather be a salesperson who can set up strong Up-Front Contracts than be a master at the art of presenting the dog-and-pony show. The contract salesperson will outperform the presenter every time. There's no doubt about it.

One final word: The most important Up-Front Contract you will ever make is with yourself. It's the contract that says nothing will drive you out of sales. This is your last professional stop!

11

STOP SELLING FEATURES AND BENEFITS

When people make decisions, they are either moving toward pleasure or away from pain. People make decisions intellectually, but they buy emotionally.

—DAVID H. SANDLER

I t sounds heretical for a sales trainer to say, "Stop selling features and benefits," doesn't it? Traditionalists have been preaching features-and-benefits selling for ages. Apparently they think it gets results, but I think it's a lot of unnecessary hard work. It's merely a safe way to sell unproductively. At best, it's arm's-length selling, and it's not effective today. Features and benefits do not lead people to make buying decisions. Features and benefits merely confuse the issue.

Try the following exercise. On a piece of paper draw a vertical line down the center of the page. At the top left side, write your company's name. Across the page, on the top right side, write the name of your major competitor. Down the left side of the page write the numbers 1, 2, and 3. Do the same thing on the right side of the page. Now, under your company's name, list the top three benefits of the product or service that you're selling. Be sure these benefits explain why people buy from you. Is it because your product or service generates increased profits? Does it maximize effectiveness or efficiency? Is it easy to use? Whatever you know the benefits to be, record them now.

I've got bad news and good news for you. If you're like most people, you want the bad news first. Here it is: you're fired.

Now for the good news: your competitor (whose name you wrote on the exercise above) just hired you!

It's your first day at work for your new boss. Go back to the right side of the paper. And under your competitor 's name (now the company you work for), record the top three benefits of the product or service that you'll be selling. When you're finished, you'll probably discover that it's difficult to distinguish between the left and right sides of the page. The benefits of your former product or service are probably not all that different from the benefits of your new product or service. Same benefits and same features.

Can you imagine sharing the results of this exercise with your prospective customers and clients? In truth, traditional salespeople do it every day. Prospects are used to hearing the same features-and-benefits presentations day after day. Chances are, each time you make a presentation, the prospect already has heard everything you're going to say ... *from the competition*! If you're selling in the traditional way, the only thing setting you apart from the competition is the company name on your business card.

If features and benefits don't convince people to buy, what does?

Traditionalists will focus on interest, arousal, and curiosity. They will appeal to the prospect's intellect, even though that's the wrong approach. They seek a prospect's interest to arouse curiosity about what their product or service can do for the prospect. That's features-and-benefits selling. And it doesn't work.

> If you're selling in the traditional way, the only thing setting you apart from the competition is the company name on your business card.

When people make decisions, they either move toward pleasure or away from pain. People make decisions intellectually, but they buy *emotionally*. Benefits such as increased profits, maximum efficiency, and ease of use appeal to the intellect but not to the emotions. Try all you want to sell intellectually; most of the time, it won't work. And when it does, it's hard work!

I suggest you choose the easy path. When you sell, pursue only the pain! *All the other emotions aren't as strong, so ignore them. Cut below the surface, uncover the prospect's real motivations, and expose the pain.*

Pain is such a strong emotion that prospects will do anything to avoid it. *When you get your prospects to feel pain, especially pain in the present, and then demonstrate that you can end their suffering and hurt, you're a step closer to the sale.*

The third compartment of the Sandler Submarine is Pain. To seal off this compartment, you have to hit your prospects right between the eyes with pain.

I've developed a five-part formula for moving through the Pain step, and it looks like this:

WELL TO *HURT* TO *SICK* TO *CRITICAL* TO *MIRACLE*

1. **Look for a *suspect* (anyone who is not yet a prospect) who is Well.** A key question to ask the Well suspect is, "How long have you had this problem?" Suspects who tell you they've had the same problem for 10 years will most likely keep the problem for another 10 years. There's no urgency here, and probably no chance of a sale either. Move on to another suspect. If, in contrast, the suspect tells you the problem has existed for a day, an hour, or perhaps even a few weeks or months, the suspect might now be ready to become a prospect.

2. **You can change your suspect to a prospect by asking questions that will cause the prospect to Hurt.** Suspects who are Well might actually see a need for your product or service. But with their guard up (not feeling any emotion), they will remain safe, secure, intellectual, in control, and unsellable. Make 'em Hurt. Explore their pain.

   Using features-and-benefits selling, the traditional salesperson tries to solve the prospect's problems too quickly. Traditionalists try to close the sale in the Hurt phase of the formula, and it rarely works.

   Soon into the Hurt phase, you'll hear the prospect say, "Can you help?" The traditionalist proudly exclaims, "You bet I can."

   But my approach, using the Dummy Curve, requires a different response. I would say, "Don't know. Can I ask you a few questions about your problem?"

   Remember, people buy emotionally, so they must *feel* their pain before the sale can be closed successfully. If you move prospects through the selling formula too quickly, you're going to lose the sale.

3. **Make your prospect Sick with pain.** Probe. Ask questions (consult Chapter 7). Soon, the prospect becomes emotionally involved in your presentation.

4. **Continue probing until you arrive at the Critical state, when prospects are willing to pay anything, do anything, to solve their suffering and hurt.** They now *feel* their problems. Critical prospects validate their own problems without interference from the salesperson. They see the need to fix the problems immediately. Their job, their business, their future, depends on eliminating the pain.

5. **Now, perform your Miracle.** Let the prospects see that your product or service can take away the pain.

Caution: While this formula is very effective, and it is used by hundreds of thousands of people who have been trained by Sandler, there's a drawback to it if you dig too deeply to expose a prospect's pain.

Some years ago, a student of ours had increased his sales productivity by 200 percent in 90 days, and he was addicted to the Pain technique. In fact, I called him a "pain animal" because he was so committed to it. One day, he pushed too far with a prospect and ultimately lost a sale that he had already closed.

Immediately following his sales meeting with the prospect, the student later told me that he was proud of the way he had handled the Pain step. "After 90 minutes of defense," he explained, "I finally cracked through the wall with this prospect. Any clinical psychologist would have been pleased with how I had stripped away the prospect's problem, layer after layer, from intellectual interest to bare-bones hurt. I got the sale."

But by the time he had returned to his office, his new client had called and left a message to cancel the order. "I could never reach him again. He wouldn't talk to me. Apparently, I had done such a good job of uncovering the prospect's pain that I embarrassed him. And I lost the sale."

Salespeople are not trained to pursue pain in the fashion of a psychologist, and I do not condone trying to do so. The Pain step was not developed for salespeople to play "low-budget shrink." However, when it's used properly, it offers the prospect more than a sales call that will merely arouse curiosity. It matches your product or service to your prospect's pain, leading to a buying decision.

By now you're probably wondering: "How do I pursue my prospect's pain?"

Let me rephrase that question for you. Ask it this way: "How do I guide my prospects to discover their own pain?"

It's important to ask the question this way because it's much easier to close a sale if the prospects have discovered their own pain rather than hearing you disclose their pain. People don't like to admit their pain. If you try to show them their pain, three things will happen:

1. They will become embarrassed by having to reveal their pain to you.
2. They will start to feel Not-OK about their pain. (Remember the Bonding and Rapport Rule about never making prospects or clients feel Not-OK?)
3. They will have to admit they made a previous faulty decision that led to their current circumstances. That hardly puts them in a buying mood!

To pursue your prospect's pain, you use a combination of human relations skills, especially *active listening* and *asking questions.* These are two of the techniques that fuel the Sandler Submarine.

How do you listen actively? Metaphorically, someone described it this way: "You are my friend when you walk in my moccasins." In other words, it's one thing to hear what a prospect says; it's quite another to understand the prospect's position, from the prospect's point of view. Active listening demands that you understand the prospect's situation or dilemma and that you convey this understanding to the prospect. Furthermore, it's important not to judge the prospect.

Active listening promotes trust, an important prerequisite if a prospect is going to reveal pain. Traditional salespeople, with their dog-and-pony shows, frequently plow ahead without much regard for the prospect. In their attempt to control the selling dance, they lose control for lack of the prospect's trust.

Here are four techniques that will help you become an active listener:

1. **Tell prospects that you understand.** You'll be surprised how quickly people will trust you when you respond to them with "I

understand." Try it. Here are several variations: "I understand what you are saying." "That makes sense." And, "That's not unusual."

> Listen for words that express the prospect's feelings.

2. **Repeat the prospect's words.** I call this "parroting." It's not as effective as "I understand," but it's still worthwhile. You'll sound like an echo when you repeat prospects' words, but it's comforting for prospects to hear a salesperson parrot them. *"You felt the directional vectors were off as a result of a bug in the program?"*

3. **Paraphrase the prospect's words.** Listen to the prospect, and then rephrase the prospect's statement in your own words. It's a good way to make sure you're hearing correctly. And it provides a little variety to paraphrase rather than parrot or continue saying that you understand. *"In other words, the computer program messed up the accuracy of the vectors?"*

4. **Provide feedback about what the prospect is feeling.** Listen for words that express the prospect's feelings. When you hear these words, store them in your memory, or take notes. Then, when appropriate, feed back the feelings. *"It sounds to me like you became frustrated with the bugs in the program."*

Try these techniques and you'll discover that your prospects will be inclined to trust you.

While listening actively, it's also necessary to ask questions to uncover a prospect's pain. Here are some generic questions that, when asked in a sales meeting, lead to discovering a prospect's pain:

> "How do you feel about that?"
> "How serious would you say the problem is today?"
> "What were you hoping I could do for you?"
> "Is there anything about your present situation you
>   don't like?"
> "What are you thinking about?"
> "What do you like about what you are currently using?"
> "What would you like to change or improve, if anything?"

"How do you see that working for you?"

"Sounds like no matter what I say or what our system can do, it wouldn't make any difference."

"Isn't what you already have doing the job?"

"How long has this been a problem?"

"What's the real problem?"

"In the industry, we've noticed a problem with [blank]. Have you experienced anything similar?"

"If you were to change today, what would you do differently?"

"Does that mean that you're not open to new ideas?"

"If you were to pick one thing that you didn't like about that, what would it be?"

"Do you have any problems in relation to [blank]?"

"How do I tell you you're making the wrong decision without your getting upset?"

"Where do you see a need for improvement?"

"When did you first decide you should look into [blank]?"

"Why am I here?"

"Good. So, what I hear you saying is that finding a better way of helping the [blank] isn't that critical. Am I right or wrong about that?"

"Why did you agree to see me?"

"How long have you been thinking about this?"

"And you never have a problem with [blank]?"

"That probably means you are happy with [blank]?"

"How much is the problem costing you?"

The list of pain-probing questions is endless, and it's important for you to develop questions that you can ask comfortably. It's a good idea to take notes when you begin asking questions. People love to be interviewed, especially if they're talking about something near and dear to them, and that certainly describes their pain! Act like a news reporter. Gather information from the prospect, and write it in your notebook.

Continue asking questions until you uncover the prospect's pain. A rule of thumb is that you'll need to ask at least three questions to get to the pain. The first two responses to your questions will result in what

I call Intellectual Smoke Screens (ISS). They're pain indicators, but they're not real pain. When you hear ISS, continue asking questions!

How will you know when you've succeeded? How will you know your prospect is in pain?

You'll know because you've never heard it before. The prospect's responses will become emotional, not intellectual. The prospect's words will be different. A prospect in pain uses words such as *worried, concerned, frustrated, wasted effort, angry, upset, afraid, lost all hope, terrible situation,* and *disappointed.*

For example, imagine an accountant calling on a prospect. The accountant asks the prospect, "How can I help you?"

The prospect says, "I would like to pay less in taxes and keep more money in my pocket." That may sound like pain, but it's an ISS. It's not an emotional response. If the accountant tries to close the sale now, it's too early. There's no pain. When the prospect says, "I'm tired of giving away my money to the government, and I'm not going to do it anymore," or something similar, with emotion, *that's* pain.

> A prospect in pain uses words such as *worried, concerned, frustrated, wasted effort, angry, upset, afraid, lost all hope, terrible situation,* and *disappointed.*

In addition to using emotional words or statements, a prospect in pain uses different body language. If the pain gets severe, the prospect may get up and walk around the room, or look out a window, almost ignoring you. Some prospects lower their heads, shake their heads, lower their eyes, or slouch in their chairs. That's when you know they're feeling pain.

It's not unusual to get excited the first few times you successfully lead a prospect through the pain discussion. After all, you know you're that much closer to the sale. But don't show your real emotions. Pain is never a pleasant experience. Your prospect shouldn't see you smiling. Take your lead from the prospect. Shake your head sympathetically. Empathize with the prospect's pain. At this point, selling is acting.

SANDLER SELLING TIP

You can't sell people anything. They must discover that they want it. Good pain questions help you define the extent of the prospect's perceived problem. Ask them!

We're often asked to condense the Sandler pain questions into a short list that's relevant and useful to each and every salesperson. Although the list of possible pain questions is endless and the specifics of your own market and your own experience should guide your discussions with prospects, we can tell you that any short list of effective initial pain questions is likely to include the following:

"Tell me more about that."
"Can you be a bit more specific? Give me an example."
"How long has that been a problem?"
"What have you tried to do about that?"
"And did that work?"
"How much do you think that has cost you?"
"How do you feel about that?"
"Have you given up trying to deal with the problem?"

—DHM

Sandler Pain Funnel

I believe in allowing the prospect to define the boundaries of the sales meeting. I believe in creating a win-win proposition in which both prospect and salesperson can get their needs met. I think prospects should have the opportunity to match their pain with a product or service and to fix their hurts. And I think salespeople should have the opportunity to capture new customers and go to the bank as often as possible.

I can live with being laid-back while the traditionalist pushes hard. I can live with helping prospects close the sale themselves while the traditionalist has to force the closing. I can live with showing my prospects empathy while the traditionalist feels pressure throughout the sales meeting. I can live with relaxing and having fun while the traditionalist must work hard to hide his tactics. I can live with disqualifying suspects early on while the traditionalist must present, present, and present to make her numbers work. I can live with developing pain while the traditionalist sells features and benefits.

Most of all, I can live with using the Sandler Submarine, feeling proud that I stayed out of the way while my prospect charted his or her own course, free to choose or reject my offer. If you can live with that, too, I suggest you turn to the next chapter!

12

RUDE TO DISCUSS MONEY? I DON'T THINK SO!

Imagine a millionaire making your sales call. Would there be any delay in getting to the point of money? Not likely. So why not adopt the same habit for yourself?

—DAVID H. SANDLER

Why is it that most people, sales professionals included, agonize about the subject of money? It's probably the most important step in the Sandler Submarine, and most salespeople will run from it. Why?

Because that's how we were taught. This time, it's not the traditional sales trainers who are to blame but the norms of our society, which were handed down to us through the generations. Think about it for a moment. During your childhood, if you were encouraged to talk about money, you were one of the few. Parents admonished their children not to talk about money: "It's rude to ask, 'How much money do you earn?' It's rude to ask anything at all about money!" And so we've been trained to dance around the issue of dollars and cents.

To become successful in sales, however, you've got to be comfortable talking about money, and if you're not, it will be obvious to your prospects. So right now, forget everything you've been conditioned to think about money. In fact, try this exercise.

> During your childhood, if you were encouraged to talk about money, you were one of the few.

Pretend you've just arrived in Times Square in New York City. In bright neon lights, right up there between the billboards for the stars of the latest hit TV shows, you see your own image and a message that reads: "I'm financially independent, and I don't need the business!"

Isn't that great! It's not meant to be arrogant. But if you could imagine yourself as financially independent, without the need for anyone's business, it would be easy to talk about money. There would be no pressure. And everyone around you would sense your comfort with the subject of money.

If you ever find yourself among a group of millionaires, you'll quickly discover that there's not a bit of hesitancy in talking about money. Self-made millionaires get into the habit of not wasting time. Imagine a millionaire making your sales call. Would there be any delay in getting to the point of money? Not likely. So why not get into that habit yourself?

Listen for Money Clues in Pain

Prospects will frequently give away some money clues during the Pain step. So it's important to listen closely.

> PROSPECT: *I've bought this kind of service before, and the problem I had was the $500 I gave to the salesperson. It never seemed to solve the problem. Is that going to be the same case with you?*

Now you know that the prospect has spent $500 on this problem before. It's always helpful to know something about a prospect's buying habits. However, the appropriate nurturing and bonding response would be this:

> SALESPERSON: *I'm not sure, Mr. Prospect. But I'm making a note of that right here. When I know a little more about your problem, I'll be able to tell you. OK?*

In other situations, you might hear that a prospect can't buy your product or service. In that event, why spend the time digging for pain?

"I know I have to fix this problem, but money is always tight." Or, "With the IRS breathing down my neck, I don't know how I'll be able to do anything about this situation I'm in."

If you hear comments like these, don't dig for pain. Instead, gently reverse the prospect by saying this:

"Interesting. Tell me more about that."

Or you could go immediately to the Negative Reverse Sell and say, "Is it over?"

If the prospect says, "Yes," then you move on.

If the prospect says, "No," then you say, "Well, it sounds like it's going to be over because if you are having trouble with the IRS, obviously you can't get rid of your pain."

One of these tactics will clarify the situation for both you and the prospect!

How often have you given a presentation to a prospect only to discover the prospect was broke? The most excited prospects, in my opinion, are usually the prospects who don't have any money. Nothing could be more discouraging!

Nowhere in this book is it more appropriate than now to say: Time is money!

It beats doing what the traditionalists do. They sell features and benefits. They rouse curiosity. They tease. They spend time building up to the wrong crescendo: the money question. They can't close without broaching the subject of money, and the prospect knows it. Consequently, the prospect doesn't pay much attention to the dog-and-pony show. Just the highlights will do. The prospect sits back and waits for the crescendo, silently thinking: "When's she going to talk about money? How much does this service cost? If it's too much, I'll have to go to the committee, and I don't know if I want to do that." When the prospect has had enough and the salesperson has yet to discuss money, the prospect will pop the question. And the traditional salesperson will be forced to scramble. Now the chase is on! How it goes depends totally upon the prospect. The traditionalist never had control of this sales call.

Who needs all that pressure and the disappointment that's likely to follow? Who needs to chase prospects to the point of exhaustion? Rather than stalling, why not ask about money up front and get it out of the way? It's so much easier to talk about money now (when the prospect doesn't expect it) than later.

If you've gone through the Pain step successfully, then you've conditioned your prospect for the Budget step. *The more pain the prospect experiences, the more money the prospect will pay for your product or services.* Money is never an obstacle for someone who's buying or not buying. Prospects who are in real pain will pay whatever it takes to get rid of the pain. To explain what I mean let me share with you a personal experience.

In 1969, about a year into my business, I was invited to deliver the keynote address at the Sheet Metal and Litho Association convention in New Orleans. The program chairperson, the president of a large sheet metal company in Baltimore, was a client of mine, so that's how I got the invitation. There were some 400 executives at this convention, and I had decided to talk to them about "What You 'R' Is Not Who You 'I'" (the I/R Theory that you read about in Chapter 3). I shared the deserted island story with the convention and led the executives through the exercise so that they could each evaluate and rank their I (identity) and their R (role).

I suggested to the attendees that when they returned home, they should lead their sales staffs through the I/R Theory, and I gave them copies of my information, along with my name and telephone number. I explained that regardless of how much training they'd done with their sales staffs, I was sure it wasn't living up to their expectations. (In fact, I knew this to be the case because my client had told me so prior to inviting me to speak. Many of the executives in the room had complained to him that in spite of spending tens of thousands of dollars on training, it didn't work. They'd get a spike in their sales productivity for a week or two, but eventually productivity would return to the status quo.)

Express Your Feelings Through Third-Party Stories

How many times have you been in front of a prospect and found yourself in a situation where you "felt" something, but were afraid to say it out loud?

For example, suppose your prospect puts a lot of pressure on you because of the price of your product or service. Rather than defending your position, you could use the third-party approach to tell your prospect how you feel:

"Kate, I appreciate your problem. Just last week, when I was working with a client, I really felt uncomfortable. What had happened was that after agreeing to a price that I went to my home office for, he changed the rules on me. It really made me feel uncomfortable. If I go to my home office and get this price for you, that won't happen with us, will it?"

Try it and see if it doesn't work!

I told the executives their traditional training methods didn't work because their salespeople were placing too much emphasis on getting their needs met, and they suffered from low self-esteem. My closing statement was an invitation for the executives to call me in Baltimore if they had any questions about the I/R Theory. And with that, I flew back home.

Since my primary source of revenue in those early days was in Baltimore, I wasn't expecting any business to come from the convention. However, two days after I had returned home, I received a call early one morning from a very excited individual, an executive from a sheet metal company in Crawfordsville, Indiana. He said we had not been introduced at the convention, so I wouldn't remember him, but when he returned home he administered the I/R Theory to his sales staff of more than 20 people, and not one scored above an I-4! He was flabbergasted. He'd spent thousands of dollars on training the R side only to ignore the critical I. He wanted to know if I could come out immediately and work with his group.

At the time, my price for a two-day training program in Baltimore was $2,500. But the minute I heard this fellow on the other end of the phone, I said to myself, "Well! Here's a bluebird." It was as though I had opened the window and in he flew. I figured that as soon as he settled down and stopped talking, I would say, "Look, I get $2,500 for a seminar, plus travel expenses, and I'm happy to come out and see you."

But he just kept on talking about how he'd spent *all* this money on traditional sales training, and I was right, and he was so *happy* he had heard me speak at the convention . . . and as he was talking, I said to myself, "I get $2,500, but I get to sleep at home every night. Maybe it's worth $500 more to sleep in a hotel. As soon as he slows down, I'll ask him for $3,000."

Still, he kept on talking about how he had purchased books and audiotapes for his sales staff and none of them worked. It seemed like he talked for an hour, but I'm sure it was only a few minutes. But by now I was thinking to myself, "You know, I will have to get on an airplane to do this seminar, and I'll have to give up some selling time, so I'll ask for another $500. I'll tell him the price is $3,500."

Finally the fellow stopped talking, and he asked, "Oh, by the way, how much is this going to cost me?"

I said, "$10,000 plus travel expenses."

He said, "Well, that's no problem. How soon can you get here?"

When I hung up the phone, I wondered to myself, "How much money did I leave on the table?"

That was a prospect in *real pain!*

As it turned out, I did two seminars for this client. I would have earned $5,000 for those two seminars in Baltimore, but the prospect's pain turned this opportunity into a $20,000 sale.

Let me ask you: *How much money are you leaving on the table?*

Are You Leaving Money on the Table?

Several years ago, I had decided to come off the road and stop doing seminars. I made the decision not to travel anymore but to spend my time building Sandler Training and expanding our franchise network. I felt that I couldn't do justice to these projects while flying around the country conducting seminars.

It had been several months since I had conducted a seminar when a fellow called our office asking to hire me. He had attended one of my seminars in the 1970s, and now he was a senior vice president of sales for a large company in Memphis, Tennessee, and he wanted me to conduct a seminar for his sales staff.

Since I was out of the office at the time, one of my associates handled the call. He explained that I was no longer doing seminars but that he, in fact, could conduct the seminar. He knew all of my material, and he was fully capable of conducting the program. My associate then proceeded to close the deal. He arranged to run a one-day training workshop in Memphis for $7,500, plus travel expenses.

Before this new client hung up, he asked my associate, "Is Sandler in the office?" It just so happened that I had walked in at that very moment, and my associate, feeling good about the sale, handed me the phone.

The fellow told me who he was, and even though I didn't remember him, he went on to relate how much he had relied on my techniques through the years. He thought my ideas had a lot of value, and he was calling because he really wanted me to conduct a seminar for his sales staff. I explained to him that I wasn't doing seminars anymore. He then asked, "Is that really true, or are you just using Negative Reverse Selling on me?"

I laughed and told him that it was true. "I just don't do programs anymore. I'm very busy with our company and my franchisees."

He was persistent, and so he asked, "Would you do the seminar for any amount of money?"

"Well, I really don't do programs anymore," I repeated. "But I don't know what 'any amount of money' means. I don't know if I would say yes or no. Why don't you take a crack at me?"

He said, "I've got $15,000 in my budget, and I'm willing to give it all to you if you'll do a one-day program in Memphis."

I said, "Done." A week later, I was in Memphis conducting a sales seminar.

That phone call taught my associate two hard lessons:

1. He lost the sale. "I never asked you to give me the phone," I said to him.
2. He left a lot of money on the table!

"You disclosed your price too soon," I explained. "Did you ask him how much money he had in his budget? It included double the amount of money you settled for."

Too many salespeople leave money on the table. Why? They sell *intellectually* and not *emotionally*. They don't develop the Pain step adequately. And they don't ask the right questions.

Traditional salespeople can't help leaving money on the table. They've been trained to "blue-sky" their product or service. They often promise more than they can deliver, and they almost always compare what they sell to what their competitors sell, as though any of this intellectual mumbo jumbo makes any difference to the prospect. ***Remember:*** People don't buy intellectually. They buy emotionally. That's why it's so important, before talking about money, to get your prospect involved in a discussion of pain.

In the Sandler Selling System, you move from a suspect to a prospect; from a prospect who's well and who doesn't need you to a prospect who's in pain, who's hurting, and who's sick. Focus on the pain until the prospect turns critical. Then perform your miracle. At that point, the prospect will pay you any amount of money to get rid of the pain.

By the way, after my experience with the client in Indiana, I never charged less than $10,000 for a two-day seminar. I wonder if I could have charged $25,000. But in 1969, after making $12,500 a year, $10,000 was a tremendous amount of money for two days' work!

So now, are you ready to discuss money with your prospect? Usually, I don't believe in preplanned scripts. For one thing, they're difficult to remember, and also, they can sound rehearsed. However, the Budget step is critical to your success in sales. Therefore, it's not a bad idea to memorize a few scripts that you can use during this process.

Three Steps to a Successful Discussion of Money

Don't wait to deal with money until the end of your sales presentation. Get the issue on the table up front.

Leave the Pain compartment of the submarine, and proceed to the Budget compartment if you've covered all of the following:

1. You have raised a sufficient number of pains in your prospect, and you have determined how much money each of these pains will cost your prospect.
2. You have reviewed the Pain step, and neither you nor your prospect has any mutual mystification as to what you are going to try to accomplish. During the review, avoid committing yourself to any solutions.
3. Your gut tells you that your prospect is real. Don't go forward if the prospect isn't being honest with you.

A good opening line for the Budget step is this: "Ms. Johnson, do you have a budget set aside for [your product or service]? Would you mind sharing it with me in round numbers?"

Leading into the Budget step, first review the Pain step with your prospect. You can say, "Mr. Smith, let me see if I have this straight. You talked about the trouble you're having with [Pain 1], [Pain 2], and [Pain 3], and it sounds like what you're hoping I can do is [Solution 1], [Solution 2], and [Solution 3]. Is that a fair statement?"

If Mr. Smith says "yes," then you very gently move into the Budget step by saying: "Well, Mr. Smith, let me ask you a question. Do you have a budget set aside for this project?" (Of course, if the prospect said "no," you would have to revisit the Pain step and clarify the issues.)

That's the easiest way to move into the Budget step. Here's an alternative approach:

"Mr. Smith, assuming that we have a fit between your problem and what I'm offering, the investment in my product [or service] is going to run between $750 and $1,000 depending on what you will need. Is that going to be a problem?"

That's easy enough, isn't it?

What can you do if talking about money makes you uncomfortable? Try this approach:

"Ms. Jones, we've discussed the problems you are having, and I'd like to show you that there's a way for my product [or service] to help you get rid of the problems. Before I do that, however, I have a problem of my own that I'd like to share with you. I am very enthusiastic about my product, and I'm sure you will see there is potentially a fit for the need you have. But my personal problem is dealing with money. It's something I'm not comfortable with. My parents always told me it wasn't polite to talk about money. So would it be OK with you if we deal with the money up front?"

This nonthreatening script clears the way for you and the prospect to discuss money.

The quickest way to move into the Budget step is to simply ask: "Do you have a budget set aside for this project?" That's direct, isn't it? But you've got to be ready for the prospect to respond in one of three ways:

1. "No, I don't have a budget." That's the response you'll hear most often, even if it's not true.
2. "Yes, I have a budget."

3. "Yes, I have a budget, but I can't share it with you. That wouldn't be fair to your competitors."

Here's how to handle each of these responses.

The "No" Response

Remember the OK/Not-OK information from Bonding and Rapport? It's important to avoid making the prospect feel uncomfortable because if he begins to feel Not-OK, he'll want to get rid of you. So here's what you say to prospects who say they don't have a budget:

"That's not unusual. *(It's a softening statement.)* How do you plan to make this investment? *(That's nurturing.)*"

It's a fair question, and the prospect's answer will be very important to you. Is the prospect fishing for information? Or is there serious intent to buy a product or service such as what you're offering?

Most likely, the prospect is going to tell you something more about how the decision will be made to purchase your product or service. You might even find out who controls the money and how much money will be available for this acquisition.

The "Yes" Response

When prospects acknowledge that indeed there is a budget set aside for the project, you respond:

"Fine. Would you mind sharing that with me in round numbers?"

Your response includes two key parts. The first is the word "sharing." Ask the prospect to share because, generally, people like to share. The word "sharing" is a psychological trigger for your prospect to open up with a piece of information.

The second key part is the phrase "round numbers." Notice how it doesn't sound threatening. Had you said, "Could you tell me *exactly* what that number is?" the prospect most likely would feel pressured and therefore threatened. At that point, the buyer-seller wall would go up, and the prospect would shut down. Suddenly, he or she doesn't feel OK. But the phrase "round numbers" is soft and easy to handle. The prospect will likely give you a number that is more specific than you could imagine.

The "I Won't Share" Response

Be careful when the prospect refuses to share the budget with you, even in round numbers. Don't attack. Don't pressure the prospect. Do you know what happened? I'm sorry to say it, but you missed something during the Pain step. You can't go through a good Pain step and then have the prospect say, "I'm not going to share the budget number with you." *Remember:* When you are thorough during the Pain step, the prospect will pay any price to fix the problem!

However, if you get the "I won't share" response, your best move is to "bracket" the prospect. Here's how it works:

"Ms. Jones, that makes sense. *(Softening statement; more bonding.)* As you can probably imagine, we have many products that might be able to solve your problem. Some of our solutions range in price from $3,000 to $9,000, and others from $9,000 to about $20,000. Now, I understand that this is confidential information. *(Softening statement.)* But off the record *(another softening statement),* should we address the 3-to-9 range, or should we go for the 9-to-20 range?"

About 80 percent of the time, according to statistics that we've gathered at our company, the prospect will steer you toward one bracket or the other. Whichever way the prospect steers you, you take the opposite approach. For example, suppose Ms. Jones says: "Well, based on what I know, we could really handle from $3,000 to $9,000."

You say: "That surprises me. I thought, because of the extent of your problems, that you were going to pick 9 to 20."

But suppose Ms. Jones says: "We could handle $9,000 to $20,000." You say: "Well, that really is interesting. I thought you were going to pick 3 to 9."

Ms. Jones wasn't expecting what you just did. You used the Dummy Curve *plus* Negative Reverse Selling!

If the bracket that the prospect selects will cover the cost of your product or service, you could continue by doing more bracketing:

"Ms. Jones, let me ask you another question. Would you say you're in the 3-to-6 range or the 6-to-9 range?"

Be careful! Bracketing is a powerful technique. Don't cross the line. Don't push too forcefully. This is one of the techniques that requires reinforcement training for you to master it. I've seen amateurs take this technique and turn it into a power play that resulted in making the prospect feel Not-OK. The professional will be gentle with the technique. Professional salespeople never forget that they are in front of a prospect for one reason only: to go to the bank. Don't forfeit the sale just to meet your needs!

SANDLER SELLING TIP

Selling is a Broadway play performed by a psychiatrist. Have you ever lost your objectivity during an exchange with a prospect or customer? It's easy to do. Buying is inevitably an emotional experience for the prospect. For the salesperson, though, it's important not to get emotionally involved in a selling situation, because your thinking can get cloudy and the quality of your decisions can get a whole lot worse. Consider the relationship between a psychiatrist and his patient. During a session, the patient suddenly leaps to his feet, grabs a letter opener from the psychiatrist's desk, and shouts, "I'm going to kill you!"

When faced with this situation, the good psychiatrist does not cry out, in response, "Why me?" Nor does he pull out his cell phone and call the police. There's no time for that!

Instead, he maintains an objective view of the situation and says, "Tom, I can see you're upset. Before you lunge at me and do something you're sure to regret, can we talk about what's upsetting you? Perhaps there's a better way to deal with whatever you're feeling. Are you open to finding out?"

The "Why me?" response is the one most likely to get the psychiatrist killed. The objective response is the one most likely to save his life.   —DHM

Before You Drop Your Price, Give Your Product Away!

One of our franchisees called me from Pittsburgh, Pennsylvania, one afternoon to discuss a proposal that a prospect had extended to him.

It turned out that the prospect had told the franchisee, "Your price is too high."

The franchisee went through all the steps that he had learned to overcome the objection, but nothing worked. Instead, the prospect said to the franchisee, "Look, I'd like you to come in next Friday and conduct some training. You said you have the time. It's only a week away, and chances are that between now and then, you are not going to get a chance to find work on that day, so why don't you come in and take the money I'm willing to give you [which was less than the franchisee's regular fee]? At least then you'll get some pay for that day."

The franchisee told the prospect, "I'll get back to you," and that's when he called me.

"You know," he said to me via telephone, "the guy has a good point. I am not going to be working on Friday. I don't have time to sell someone else some training because it's only a few days away. Why not take the money the prospect offered me, and at least I'll put some money in the bank?"

In spite of what I knew he wanted me to tell him, this is what I said:

"It would be a mistake to do that because you're working on the wrong end of the problem. First, you missed something during the Pain step. That's why the prospect balked at your price. But now, if you drop your price, you're going to mess up your head. You're going to work for less than what I am saying you are worth. Pretty soon, you are going to think you're worth less, and the lower price will become your real price."

Then I gave him an alternative:

"Go back to your prospect, and tell him you can't drop your price, but you will do the work for nothing. That way, both of you can get your needs met. He will get his training, which will take care of some of his sales problems, and you will feel good about yourself because you didn't drop your price. And then, when you go on your next call, you'll do a better Pain step, and you'll ask for the money and get it."

So the franchisee went back to the prospect and said, "You know, I thought about your offer, and it isn't the money. I just don't want to mix up my head. I'll do the job for you anyway, pro bono." During my active selling years, I did a lot of work pro bono simply because the prospect needed me and couldn't afford me. It was better to give the work away than to end up feeling Not-OK. Oftentimes, the free work resulted in thousands of dollars of revenues that I wouldn't have otherwise received.

By the way, when my franchisee went back to the prospect and offered to do the work for free, the prospect changed his mind. He paid the full price for the training! Upon reflection, the prospect was afraid he wouldn't get first-class treatment if he forced the franchisee to work for free.

What if the prospect's bracket is too low and there doesn't appear to be enough money to afford your product or service? In that event, here are the questions you should ask:

> "What will you do if the investment is higher than you planned for?"
> "In case we can't go first class, are there some problems we can trim if we have to? Which ones?"
> "Are you really committed to solving these problems?"

The "That Could Be a Problem" Reverse

You might find the "That could be a problem" Reverse to be especially useful at times when the prospect doesn't appear to have enough money to buy your product or service. Here's how it works:

SALESPERSON: *Do you have a budget set aside for this project?*

PROSPECT: *Yes.*

SALESPERSON: *Would you share it with me in round numbers?*

PROSPECT: *It's somewhere between $500 and $1,000.*

SALESPERSON: *Hmm. That could be a problem. . . . What are you planning to do if the investment needs to be higher?*

This same reverse is useful even when the prospect's budget will cover the cost of your product or service. Let's say your product sells for $750. The prospect's budget is in the range of $500 to $1,000.

"Hmm. That could be a problem."

You deliberately make it appear as though the higher number won't cover the cost of the product, even though you know it will. Later, when you deal specifically with the price, $750 will look good to a prospect who thought that $1,000 would not be enough.

The Monkey's Paw Technique

If you sell a big-ticket item, money is very likely a stumbling block in your sales efforts. If that's the case, you might find a Monkey's Paw to be helpful.

If you've ever watched a cruise ship come into dock, you might have noticed the huge ropes that tie the ship to the dock. The ropes are about as thick as a grown man's arm, and they're heavy. How do they get those ropes from the bow of the ship—about 10 stories high—to the pier? They use what's called a Monkey's Paw. There's no way to throw that rope from the bow to the pier without some help. And the help is a tiny rubber ball, tied to a long string, tied to a big rope. A member of the ship's crew throws the ball to a dockhand on the pier, and the dockhand pulls the ball, the string, and the heavy rope to the dock!

So what's that got to do with helping you make more money in sales? If you sell a big-ticket item, it might be difficult for your prospect to make an all-or-nothing decision because of your price. But what if you were to break up your price into little prices?

For instance, could you sell a research project, or a study? Is there a one-day consulting project you could do? Is there a 30-day trial you could sell? Ask yourself what you could sell that would be significantly less costly than the total cost of your product or service. Your prospect might not be able to afford the total cost. Or perhaps the prospect can't fund the entire project without going to a committee. Your prospect might, however, be ready to spend a smaller amount of money. So throw out a Monkey's Paw. Get a little piece of the action, and then progressively help yourself to more of it.

Another advantage of the Monkey's Paw is that it frequently takes your competition off the street! Once a client makes a small investment with you, even against a larger investment, and providing that you do your job satisfactorily, or your product performs up to par, it's not likely that the client will give the business to a competitor. Give the client the opportunity to apply the small investments toward the big-ticket price, and you're likely to lock up the business.

Years ago, Trane Air Conditioning was one of my clients, and I introduced the Monkey's Paw to the company's sales force. They were selling multi-million-dollar air-conditioning units, which they called "chillers." These are the huge units that sit on top of the roofs of hospitals and hotels. They had a problem because the selling cycle was long, usually six to eight months (it's a big decision to spend a few million bucks!), and also, they had to compete against two or three larger competitors.

One of Trane's salespeople participated in the Sandler reinforcement training program, the President's Club, and one day he explained how "the big boys," his competitors, were beating him to the sale. That ended when he created a Monkey's Paw!

First, he wrote a very sophisticated questionnaire, including some 40 checkpoints. After that, he explained to his prospects that he could conduct a study for them. He would walk through the prospect's building with his questionnaire, gather the necessary data, and then provide an objective analysis, in writing, of the prospect's needs. The study would advise the prospect about the type of unit that would be most appropriate for the building. Best of all, the study cost only $750! That price sounded reasonable to someone who eventually would have to spend millions of dollars.

Suddenly, instead of going out and working on million-dollar sales, this fellow was now looking first for a $750 sale, a Monkey's Paw, to be followed by the larger investment. Of course it worked. The $750 study, while valuable in its own right, was a foot in the door. It helped the salesperson bond with the client, and as long as he delivered what he promised, he got most of the business. Eventually, Trane invited me to teach the technique (and the entire Sandler Selling System) to its national sales force.

Don't Get in the Way of Your Sale

One of the other issues that salespeople struggle with in the Budget step is the *affordability* of their product or service. Salespeople who sell a product or service that they can't personally afford frequently have trouble talking about money. Because their product is too expensive for them, they assume it's too expensive for their prospects. A good rule of thumb to remember is this: *never look in your prospect's pocket.* Don't presuppose that your product or service is expensive.

You're selling BMWs, and the average price is $55,000. Besides the company car, which costs you nothing, you own your spouse's 10-year-old Chevy, worth a few hundred dollars. Your prospect has enough pain to move to the Budget step, but you choke. Why? Because you think that spending $55,000 for a car is extravagant. Your "customer empathy" shows all over your face, and suddenly the only thing in the way of making the sale is you. Don't project a poor self-image to your prospect. *Get out of the way of the sale.* Let your prospects buy your product or service because it satisfies their pain. Learn that, and you'll go to the bank more often!

When your prospects are *really* in pain, it's not rude to talk about money. In fact, it would be rude not to!

SANDLER SELLING TIP

Don't be afraid to talk about money. One of the major differences in the Sandler Selling System is that the Money/Budget step comes relatively early in the process. Most traditional selling processes either put a wishy-washy Money step in Qualification, or they deal with money during the presentation. With Sandler, the presentation is almost the last thing you do, and the discussion about money is always a two-way dialogue that happens earlier in the process.

If you're ever tempted to uncover the money available during your presentation, as your PowerPoint slides are flashing by, stop and think about how that traditionally plays out. You're huffing and puffing to do a 60-minute presentation, and at the 45-minute mark, you unveil the overall pricing model, which is so complex no one can understand it. How unproductive is that? Then you get ready to finish the presentation and you start saying things like, "Well we're going to give you A, and we're going to give you B, and we're going to add C onto it. . . ." You're hoping to build the product or service up to make the prospect think, "Wow! That must cost a fortune!" And at the very end you get to the magic slide that reveals the magic price, which hopefully will be much lower than the prospect expected.

How well is that working for you? My guess is that it generates a response like: "This is a lot to think about. Let us get a committee together so we can study it, and we'll get back to you as soon as we figure this out."

Lots of salespeople have a "See no evil, hear no evil, say no evil" mentality when it comes to money. We refer to this as the "hope and pray" method. They go through the selling process praying that a big problem with money doesn't come up, but it usually does.

I don't know about you, but I've been selling for 25 years, and money is *always* an issue. You've got to make sure that the prospect feels comfortable with the value. And yes, you've got to have that discussion ahead of time.

How effective is this approach? Here's a true story about my teenage son Connor. Connor has been exposed to the Sandler principles for years. One Sunday afternoon, I asked him to mow the lawn. I told him exactly how I wanted it done, when I wanted him to start, and when I wanted him to finish. As the Sandler-trained salesperson he was and is, Connor let me do the talking for a while, then calmly asked: "Shall we talk about money, Dad? What are you thinking?" Yes, he talked about money early. And yes, I paid. —DHM

13

QUALIFY YOUR PROSPECT'S DECISION-MAKING ABILITY

It's OK for a prospect to tell me yes, and it's acceptable for a prospect to tell me no, but "I want to think it over" is a response that I simply won't tolerate. I suggest you adopt this same policy.

—DAVID H. SANDLER

One of the things I hated most about traditional selling was the pressure it created in my life. Invariably I would make a presentation only to wonder: "Will I get a yes or a no?" If the prospect wanted to "think it over," how long would it take to get a decision? And would the decision be favorable or not? If the decision wasn't favorable, had I done something wrong during the sales discussion? And if I didn't get a yes, would I be able to meet my monthly expenses without that much-needed commission? All this added up to pressure, *lots* of pressure.

> Unfortunately, most salespeople externalize the pressure related to decision making by getting angry at the prospect.

Perhaps you know exactly what I mean. You've probably given up a few weekends to prospects. You made a presentation on Friday, and the prospect said, "Call me Monday, and I'll give you my decision. I need to think it over." All weekend, instead of relaxing with your family and friends, you worried about your prospect's decision and the likelihood of your hearing a yes on Monday and collecting a fat commission check on payday. And what happened on Monday? The prospect wouldn't even answer his phone. That's pressure!

Unfortunately, most salespeople externalize the pressure related to decision making by getting angry at the prospect. In truth, the problem isn't the prospect. It's the salesperson. Traditionally, salespeople have been taught to make the presentation first and ask for the decision last. And that's what creates the pressure. It's far better to qualify the prospect's decision-making abilities *prior* to making the presentation.

If the prospect doesn't qualify, you can decide not to deliver the presentation and spare yourself the pressure.

If the prospect doesn't qualify and you decide to deliver the presentation anyway, at least you know what to expect, and you still can avoid the pressure.

If the prospect *does* qualify, you may never have to deliver the presentation because qualified prospects tend to close themselves. And, believe me, there's no pressure in that!

SANDLER SELLING TIP

Titles are no indication of decision-making ability. Selling is a development process that is driven by you, the seller. One of the most important decisions you must make is when to disengage because you haven't qualified the decision maker!

When it comes to buying decisions, you really do have to confirm who makes them, where are they made, how are they made, and so on. You can't assume anything. Even if you track down someone's title online, even if you see that someone has a corner office, you can't assume that person is going to make the decision on his or her own. You have to deal with the decision process as it actually exists, and that means you have to do some digging. If you do decide to stay in the game, it should be because you have a clear picture of all the formal and informal elements that will go into a final decision to buy or not to buy.

The Pain, Budget, and Decision steps make up Sandler's Qualifying stage. Not everyone deserves a presentation. Even a person with an impressive-sounding title may not deserve a presentation! It's your job to make sure you are working with people who are *able and willing* to move forward with you if they love what you have to say. That means you have to do a lot more than a Google search on your primary contact's name!   —DHM

By the way, I think it's important to emphasize that I didn't learn these lessons in an ivory tower or in a week's time. The Sandler Submarine evolved one compartment at a time as I experimented in the field calling on prospects and customers. If there was something about the sales process that disturbed me, I analyzed it and tried to figure out a way to resolve it. Hearing a prospect say "I want to think it over" really disturbed me. I eventually discovered that I could resolve that problem by refusing to accept that response. That's when I created the Decision compartment of the submarine. And that's when pressure ceased to exist in my selling experiences.

It's OK for a prospect to tell me yes, and it's acceptable for a prospect to tell me no, but "I want to think it over" is a response that I simply won't tolerate. I suggest you adopt this same policy. If you do, you'll discover that your prospects will respect your policy, and even better, they'll respect you for taking this position. I learned the latter part of this lesson at a company in York, Pennsylvania.

Many years ago, not long after I had created the Decision compartment of the submarine, I was contacted by a company in York, about an hour's drive from my home. The company had received a brochure about my sales training workshops, and the vice president of training asked that I visit them and meet with their executive team.

Before I agreed to the sales call, I qualified the prospect on the telephone. He verified that he would attend the presentation personally, and he also confirmed that he would be able to say yes or no at the end of my presentation. With this Up-Front Contract in place, I made the trip to York.

Guess what happened when I visited the company? I made my presentation, and the vice president of training said he would not make a decision after all. And would I return the next day after he had a chance to "think it over" and consult with another member of the company?

The easiest thing was to bail out at this point, let the prospect off the hook, and return the next day. This was not a small account. I was looking at big bucks if I got the business. A part of me said, "OK, the guy blew some smoke. Why not just agree to return tomorrow?" But the smarter part of me said, "Hold it! Be true to your system."

In these types of situations, I have learned that it's more important to protect your value system—protect your I (identity) and your R (role) and everything that you believe in professionally—than to help the prospect feel better or even to get the business.

So when the vice president of training asked me to return the next day, I said that I would not. "There should be no misunderstanding about the agreement that we had," I said as I sat among the company's executives in the conference room. "I am happy to stay here today as long as it takes to show you how I am going to help you with your problems, but since you had agreed to say yes or no at the end of my presentation, we will either start or not start with my program. I'll leave you and your people alone, and I'll sit outside your conference room and wait for a yes or no. If you can't say yes today, I'll take a no." And then I got up and left the room.

For an hour I waited outside the conference room until they called me back into the meeting. They had arrived at a decision, and it was yes. I thanked them for the business, and then I said, "I would like to know how you made the decision."

The vice president of training went to the blackboard and showed me that they had used the traditional "Ben Franklin close." On one side of the blackboard they had listed all the reasons why they should buy my program. On the other side they had listed all the reasons why they shouldn't buy. There were 12 reasons why they should and 11 reasons why they shouldn't. The twelfth reason, which favored purchase, clinched the deal for me. It said, "Because he was true to his system. He won't let us fail."

By holding my ground and forcing the company to make a decision, as the vice president of training had previously agreed to, I gained the respect of the prospect, and they became my client. Whatever sales process you're committed to, I advise you to trust it. It's more important to protect what's between your ears than what might go into your wallet!

People Don't Make Decisions at the Same Time, All the Time

I learned a lot about how people make decisions in the early years of my career as a workshop leader. I used to conduct daylong sales training workshops for which I charged $95 to $275 per person, depending on the subject matter. My goal was to break even on the front end of the workshop but make money on the back end, where I sold memberships in my weekly training program, which I called the President's Club. A President's Club membership cost several thousand dollars. (Do you recognize this technique? It's the Monkey's Paw, which I described in Chapter 12.)

During the workshops, I introduced the participants to the basic tenets of what would later become known as the Sandler Selling System. I was up front about my intentions. I explained to the workshop audience that I planned to spend the day teaching them certain aspects of my system, and then, at about 4 p.m., I planned to ask them if they wanted to join the President's Club. I explained that for the price of membership, they would receive an audiotape library and unlimited access to the President's Club meetings. I also explained that the President's Club meetings would provide the reinforcement training that they would need to become super salespeople.

It became my practice to show up for the workshop about an hour early to set up the room. Some of the most interested participants arrived early, and I soon realized that these people were excellent prospects for the President's Club at the 4 p.m. close. One day the thought occurred to me that these early arrivals had, in fact, already made the decision to invest in the President's Club. Some people make decisions on the spot; others like to think things over. So I began to experiment with this idea.

At about 9:30 a.m., after I had already explained my intentions, and about half an hour into the workshop, I discussed the decision-making process of my system. I explained that I happen to be a quick decision maker. If I like something, I want to buy it right away. The longer a product is withheld from me, the more bored I become. And then I demonstrated the concept. I said, "For instance, some of you came to the workshop anticipating that it was something more than just a one-day opportunity for $95. Can I see a show of hands of those people who already have decided to spend more money if you like what you see, and join the President's Club?"

Depending on the size of the audience, a few hands would go up, usually three or four. At that point, I took the President's Club package and gave it to each of these people in exchange for their credit cards. And that's how I found out that you can close some sales early, even before people have seen the presentation!

About two and a half hours into my workshop, just before lunch, I introduced the "Early Bird close." I said, "Now that you've been here most of the morning and you're getting ready to go to lunch, how many people have decided to invest in the President's Club? By the way, if you make the decision before you go to lunch, you can save $50 on the membership." Another six or seven hands would go up, and I would pass out the President's Club package and take their credit cards. As a surprise, I also gave a $50 discount to the people who had signed up first thing in the morning. (Of course, I hadn't processed the orders yet, so the discount was easy to apply.) During lunch, I always remained in the room because some people would return early, having decided during lunch that they wanted to invest in the President's Club.

Surprisingly, after lunch, no matter how hard I tried to close, there were no more takers until 4 p.m. The people who hadn't already decided waited until the close of the workshop to make their decision. These were obviously the people who needed to see the entire presentation.

At 4 p.m., I asked the people who had joined the President's Club to stay after the workshop so that I could show them how to begin using the material and to give them the schedule of the President's Club meetings in their area. I also asked those who hadn't yet decided if they would join to stay behind. The remainder of the people, those who knew they were not going to join the President's Club, no matter what, were excused. I thanked them and waited for them to leave. But one or two of them always asked to stay behind because they wanted yet another opportunity to say yes or no.

At that point, I went around the room and used the Thermometer technique with those who were still undecided (see Chapter 14). "What do you have to see to get to 10?" I asked. As they told me, I fulfilled their needs to the best of my ability, and I proceeded to close the majority of the undecideds who had stayed behind.

These exercises proved to me that you never know for sure when your prospect has decided to buy. **Remember:** People don't make decisions at the same time, all the time!

By risking getting a no, you're going to get many more noes than you've heard in the past. But the good news is that you're going to get equally more yeses, and you're not going to accept "I want to think it over." The weekends, forevermore, will belong to you and your family, the way it should have been all along.

If your prospect has shared pain with you, and you've confirmed that the prospect has the money to get rid of the pain, you've now got to help the prospect decide to spend the money to get rid of the pain. This is not the time to wimp out. You've already spent half an hour going through the Pain step, and another five minutes nailing down the budget, so now spend five more critical minutes developing the Decision step of your contract.

SANDLER SELLING TIP

Keep the prospect OK throughout the sales process. In order to complete the Decision step, or indeed any other step, you must continue to keep the prospect feeling OK about talking to you (by means of establishing and reestablishing Bonding and Rapport), and you must keep each side clear about what is happening next and why (by means of new, mutually acceptable Up-Front Contracts). Typically, this means you must make sure you have consistent face-to-face contact, as opposed to a stream of disembodied email messages.   —DHM

Once you've arrived at the Decision step, it's important to review the Pain and Budget steps before you proceed. Remember, your prospects have been trained for years to mislead you. Take the time now to validate what you believe to be true in your interaction with the prospect. You might say something like this:

"Henry, what you are hoping that I can do for you is to get rid of [state his pain, or pains]. Is that a fair statement?" If the prospect agrees that the statement is fair, you've strengthened the agreement between the two of you. If the prospect says the statement isn't fair, rework it until it's clear. You may need to dig deeper for pain. Don't move on until you've got a clear understanding. Remember, no mutual mystification!

Next, review the Budget step:

"And you said, Henry, that assuming I can do this for you, in your budget there's somewhere between $1,000 and $2,000 to get rid of the pain. That's also a fair statement, isn't it?"

Make sure the prospect has the money before you proceed.

If you're in a long-cycle business, requiring multiple follow-up sales calls, it's particularly important to validate your assumptions with the prospect at each new meeting. For example:

"Mary, the last time we talked, we discussed [Pain 1, Pain 2, and Pain 3]. Is that correct? Have any other pains come to the surface since I saw you last?"

In the next discussion, you might say: "Mary, at our last meeting, not only did we discuss [state her pain or pains] but we also discussed a budget of between $95,000 and $140,000. Is that right?"

The idea is to review and validate the Pain and Budget steps in each subsequent discussion. Now you're ready to tackle the Decision step.

SANDLER SELLING TIP

The news story approach. Does the information you now obtain about your prospect's decision-making process pass the news story test? A good news story reveals the following information:

What
- What does the process involve?
- What are the specific steps?
- What specifically will he or she be listening and looking for?

When
- By when does the prospect want or need to complete the purchase?
- By when must the decision be made in order to meet any implementation and delivery deadlines?

How
- How will the ultimate decision be made?
- Where in the organization are decisions made? (At what level?)
- Where geographically are decisions made?

Who
- Who is involved in the decision-making process (and what is each person's role)?
- Who can influence the decision?
- Who has final buying authority?
- Who has veto power?

Why
- Why does the prospect make decisions in this manner?

—DHM

The News Story Approach

Get to the heart of your prospect's decision-making process by asking the following questions.

Ask the "What" Qualifier

"Jim, what decision-making process do you go through when deciding on a purchase like this one?"

Ask the "When" Qualifier

"When do you see yourself moving forward with this project, Jim?"

Don't be surprised if the prospect's time frame doesn't match your time frame. He might be a month away from making a decision, and you want the decision today. She might want to make the purchase tomorrow, but you can't deliver for 60 days. Whatever the case, you might as well dig your heels in now and deal with the issues.

Ask the "How" Qualifier

"Assuming that you want to move forward, how is it going to happen? Do I get a purchase order? A check? Or how exactly does that happen?"

You can't go to the bank without money, so find out how you're going to get it.

Ask the "Who" Qualifier

"Jim, who besides you will be involved in the decision-making process?"

A key phrase in this qualifier is "who besides you." The phrase grants the position that the prospect is involved in the decision-making process, and that's a stroke. The phrase grants the individual power, regardless of reality. Always assume the prospect will be included in the decision-making process, even if that's not to be the case.

When prospects tell you that they can make the decision solo, be careful. Check it out! Prospects have been telling salespeople for ages that they can make decisions when, in fact, they can't. Prospects don't necessarily understand verbal contracts, so here's a technique that you can use to nail down the truth:

PROSPECT: *No problem. I can make decisions myself.*

SALESPERSON: *Fine, but you mean you don't get help from a president, a committee, or a spouse?*

That gentle reverse will help many prospects to suddenly remember that indeed there are other people involved in the decision-making process:

PROSPECT: *Well, what I meant was that I make the final decision, but I do give my people a chance to express themselves.*

Ask the "Why" Qualifier

"Jim, I'm curious. Why did you choose this decision-making process?"

The Intermediate Decision-Making Technique

Now's the time to find out just who the other people are. See if you can include the others in your meeting before you move into the Fulfillment step. Consider arranging another meeting date to include the others. If you can't involve the others, then the Intermediate Decision-Making technique will be helpful. Here's how it works:

Acknowledge that the prospect will gather information from you and then report to "the committee" of decision makers. Be willing to oblige the prospect, but first, ask this question:

"Mr. Smith, I understand that you won't be making the decision on your own, and you would like me to give you the presentation, which I'm happy to do. But let me ask you this: After I give you my presentation, would you be nice enough to tell me if you would buy my product [or service] if the decision were up to you?"

What you're doing is giving your prospect a psychological baton of power—the power to say yes or no. Now, go ahead and make your presentation. And then say:

"Mr. Smith, we've covered a lot of ground today, but based on what you've seen, would you buy my product [or service] if it were up to you?"

If the prospect says no, you can bet the committee will say no too.

If the prospect says yes, you now have a better-than-even chance at getting an affirmative decision from the committee. Don't bank the commission, however.

The Rehearsal Technique

Help your prospect organize his or her presentation to the decision makers. By rehearsing your prospect's presentation, you can actually teach your prospect how to sell your product (or service) to the committee. You have a lot riding on your prospect's ability to understand everything that's necessary to know to satisfy the committee's curiosity. So, after your prospect agrees that he or she would buy your product (or service), you say, "I appreciate that, Mr. Smith. The committee [it could be a spouse, partners, or some other group] is going to ask you questions about my product [or service]. Based on what you know about the committee, what type of questions do you think you will be asked?"

Your job now is to teach your prospect as much as possible about your product or service. Go over the questions that are likely to surface during the Pain step. You'll have to help your prospect view pain through the eyes of the committee members since pain is a personal issue. You'll also need to review the issue of money. Whatever you do, don't send an ill-prepared prospect to the committee.

One silent advantage that you'll have in your favor when the prospect goes before the committee is that baton of power. The prospect already told you he would buy your product or service if he had the decision-making power. Assuming the prospect isn't blowing smoke, his ego is on the line with you. How can he tell you he would buy your product and then come back and tell you the committee said no? Ego pressure might just swing the vote your way!

Don't Get Mad at a Prospect Who Did Something You Didn't Tell Him He Couldn't Do!

Up front, before you begin your presentation, tell your prospect that it's OK to say "Yes," and it's OK to say "No," but it's not OK to say "I want to think it over."

If you don't make that clear to your prospect, you can't blame the prospect for doing what you didn't tell him he couldn't do.

If you are certain that your prospect is, in fact, the sole decision maker, then your final question in the Decision step should sound like this:

"Gina, there are three things you can say to me today. You could say no, and, of course, what that means is you have no interest in my product [or service], and I appreciate your seeing me, and I'll be out of here in just a few minutes. On the other hand, you could say yes, and what that means is that you have some interest in my product [or service] and you would like to see a presentation to make sure my product [or service] will solve your problem. Or you could say some form of 'I want to think it over.' What I suggest is that a no is OK, a yes is OK, but what shouldn't happen is for you to tell me you want to think it over. Is that something you can handle without feeling any pressure?"

If, prior to the Decision step, your prospect already agreed to reply with a yes or a no, then you simply need to review that information at this point.

If there's ever a time to be careful in the Sandler Submarine, it's in the Decision compartment. You can always handle a pain that comes up during your presentation, a few dollars one way or the other that were glossed over during the Budget step, but if you give the prospect an out in the Decision compartment, it will come back to bite you every time.

PROSPECT: *Well, I sure do want to get rid of my problems, and the money isn't the issue, but I don't want to make a hasty decision.*

This was the prospect who told you, "I can make the decision myself." Perhaps you forgot to ask the prospect, "I know you *can* make the decision, Henry, but *will* you?" Be very careful. Be professional, be patient, listen with your ears, your eyes, your heart, and your gut.

And don't wimp out! If you do, all you'll get are prospects who tell you they need to "think it over." All that adds up to is *lots* of pressure, and not many trips to the bank.

Force the Decision step before you proceed!

14

FULFILL THE CONTRACT AND LET THE PROSPECT CLOSE THE SALE

Remember, the prospect isn't interested in you. Prospects are always only concerned about how you can make their pain disappear.

—DAVID H. SANDLER

As you move through the compartments of the Sandler Submarine, you will establish a binding and mutually acceptable contract with your prospect, even though the prospect may not realize it. The exciting point is that the prospect always appears to be in control of the sales process, and therefore he or she doesn't hesitate to close the sale if the contract has been clearly defined.

Every contract must contain the following steps: Pain, Budget, and Decision. Once these three compartments of the submarine have been sealed off, all that remains is the presentation, or "Fulfillment" of the contract. And then, it's off to the bank!

Fulfillment is the sharp edge of communication. It's direct and immediate, and oftentimes, there's no second chance. How you deliver your presentation can make or break the sale. Unfortunately, many salespeople freeze at just the thought of delivering a presentation. To avoid that problem, I stress the importance of practicing the Fulfillment step as frequently as possible.

A good presenter inspires respect, confidence, credibility, and belief, and that's a tall order for even the most savvy of sales professionals. However, the Sandler approach to the presentation is easy to understand and grasp. Once you accomplish it, the Fulfillment step will satisfy your ego as much as anything else you do in the sales profession.

The following are the steps you need to take to turn yourself into a professional presenter.

Prepare for the Presentation

If you've been taking notes during the sales call, you have in front of you much of the information that you'll need to deliver your winning presentation. Hopefully, you have prioritized the notes—especially the pains that the prospect revealed—and you now know what you need to say to move this conversation to closure.

Take a moment to reflect on the prospect's pains, and decide what you want to say about each pain. Don't be concerned about making logical connections between the pains—those connections may have no significance at all to the conversation. Just be sure that whatever you decide to say does, in fact, relate to a specific pain. This isn't the time for you to raise new obstacles to closure. However, if you rushed through the Pain step, you can almost bet that your prospect will introduce some new objections.

Structure the Presentation

Like a good mystery novel, Fulfillment should include a beginning, a middle, and an end. However, be concerned about time. How much time will you have to make your presentation? Whether it's 10 minutes or an hour, you want to finish early. If you believe you'll be short on time, focus on the major pains expressed by your prospect, and make your points as quickly and sparingly as possible.

The Beginning

Begin by reviewing the many conclusions and agreements that you arrived at with your prospect as you moved through the submarine. Before you continue, make sure you have 100 percent agreement from your prospect on these issues: Pain, Budget, and Decision. For example:

"John, you told me that your major problem in building your business is getting enough good clients. You said, in fact, that you need to find one new client monthly to meet the goals that you've set for yourself in your business plan. Is that correct?"

If John doesn't say "yes," you can't proceed because you apparently missed his major problem—his primary pain—or he misled you in some way. So clarify now.

Assuming John says "yes," you would continue:

"OK, John, you also told me that you've budgeted $5,000 this year to help you solve this problem, even though you said you don't know what the solution might be. You said you might use the money to hire someone who can help you get more clients, or you might use it for sales and motivational seminars. That's accurate, isn't it?"

Again, if John doesn't say, "Yes, that's fair," find out what is fair, and then proceed.

"You also told me, John, that you've got half of the budgeted $5,000 in your checking account, and you could charge $2,500 on your Visa card—which you were also nice enough to tell me that you're carrying with you now. Am I still correct?"

John says "yes," and you continue:

"I also asked you how you would make the decision to solve this problem, didn't I? You told me that you are the sole decision maker, and you don't need to talk this over with someone else. And we agreed, didn't we, that it's OK for you to tell me 'no' today, and it's OK for you to say 'yes.' But what we don't want to do is spend this time together and say 'I've got to think it over.' That's not acceptable. In other words, you will make the decision today. Am I right about all of that?"

Be careful! Like so many prospects, John doesn't really understand what it means to make a commitment to a salesperson. Even though he has agreed to what appears to be a good Up-Front Contract, he believes he has the right to change his mind. After all, it's only a salesperson he's talking to! So if there's any doubt in your mind about John's commitment, check it out again:

"We don't want to spend all this time together, John, and then you say that someone else needs to be involved in the decision or you need to think it over. Should we spend a little more time talking about that?" You might be pushing it, but it's better to talk it out now than to go through the Fulfillment step for nothing!

Once you and your prospect agree to this verbal contract, you're ready to move into the midsection of your presentation. Just don't proceed without a clear understanding of your contract. To do so would be a fatal mistake.

Four Mistakes to Avoid During the Fulfillment Step

These four fatal mistakes will result in an unsuccessful Fulfillment step. Avoid them!

1. Failure to review the contract with the prospect prior to beginning the presentation
2. Failure to identify the prospect's pain
3. Failure to clarify the issue of money
4. Failure to get the prospect's agreement about the decision

The Middle

Now is the time to talk about the features and benefits of your product or service. Use them to drive home how you can solve the prospect's pain. Go ahead and demonstrate your product knowledge—this is your opportunity to show and tell. Show the prospect everything there is to see about your product or service that relates to the pains the prospect has expressed. Tell everything that's relative too. Minimize your use of Sandler techniques at this point. There shouldn't be much need to reverse or strip-line now. However, if your product or service includes some bells and whistles that don't relate to the prospect's pain, use the Dummy Curve to introduce them. No use talking about a feature or benefit that's not relevant—it might sabotage the sale.

Give the prospect the opportunity to touch your product, if that's possible. Touching helps your prospect experience ownership. If the product is complicated, you should find a way to let your prospect operate it. Prospects will not tell you they're uncomfortable. They'll say "no" to you instead. Remember, people want to feel OK.

If you have several pains to present, start with the one that's most bothersome to your prospect. By doing so, it's possible that you won't have to finish your presentation. Get the major objection out of the way, and your prospect may not care about anything else. Remember, you do not have to finish the presentation. Your goal is to get an order, not to win an Academy Award for best presenter.

Caution: For lack of preparation and focus, salespeople have a tendency to ramble in the midsection of the presentation. You should avoid doing that. You already established the theme of your Fulfillment exercise in the beginning of your presentation. Stick to it. Don't raise new issues. Don't drift. Maintain good eye contact with your prospect. Say as much as you have to, but be brief, simple, and direct. Take control, but don't get carried away with yourself.

Remember, the prospect isn't interested in you. Prospects are always only concerned about how you can make their pain disappear. To keep that singular focus, imagine that you see the question "What's in it for me?" imprinted on the prospect's forehead.

By the way, it's OK to be humorous in your presentation, but there are many different standards of humor, and what's funny to you may not be funny to your prospect. Unless you're certain the humor will work, you're better off not using it. Misguided humor could end a presentation prematurely.

As quickly as possible in the midsection of your presentation, get the prospect involved. Use the Reversing techniques you learned earlier to engage conversation. As soon as the prospect interrupts you, or responds to you, stop! Don't talk. You already know what you're going to say. It's far more important to know what's on the prospect's mind. Perhaps you'll discover the sale has been closed and there's no need to continue. Incidentally, prospects won't always interrupt you verbally. Be alert for body motion. Shaking the head, or crossing the arms, or looking away from you may each mean something significant. Take a pause, and give the prospect an opportunity to speak.

SANDLER SELLING TIP

Don't be afraid to abort! If you suspect your prospect isn't being honest with you, or if for some reason you believe you're getting the runaround (such as being asked to email your presentation to people who were supposed to be on hand to make a decision), simply abort your presentation.

"Well, Sarah, based on what you've said, I don't see any sense in continuing." Begin to pack up and leave. If that's what Sarah prefers, she's going to let you go. In that case, you're better off moving on to the next *real* prospect.

If your presentation starts going down the wrong track, for whatever reason, abort. Live to sell another day! —DHM

If the prospect asks you a question, don't repeat it just to buy time. My grandfather was famous for using that trick.

"Pop, how much is 2 and 2?" I'd ask him.

"How much is 2 and 2? Well, that is a very good question. The answer is that 2 and 2 always makes 4."

As a kid, I didn't recognize my grandfather's method. However, he was an uneducated farmer from the old country, and he knew how to buy time when he needed it. In front of your prospect, however, that method would look obvious, so don't use it. If you're asked a question and you don't have the answer at your fingertips, don't respond. Keep quiet and let your subconscious work. Whatever you say next will sound better than if you had repeated the prospect's question.

The midsection of Fulfillment requires patience and caring. Rushing to get through the compartment—rather than listening and waiting—will almost always result in a no-sale.

The End

While it's wise not to rush the Fulfillment step, it's important to finish as quickly as possible and still get the sale. The sooner you successfully seal off this compartment, the sooner you've got the sale. However, it's not easy to know when to conclude your presentation.

Let's assume that you have five pains to solve during your presentation. You begin with the most troublesome pain first and explain how your product or system can alleviate the problem. You then say:

"John, are you 100 percent comfortable that my service will solve the problem?"

You must get a yes from John, or you're giving him an out to fall back on later. Without applying pressure, gently find out what's keeping John from agreeing that the service will solve his problem. You're stuck until you get his complete agreement. So give him time to raise the objections. If you were thorough in the Pain compartment of the submarine, and if John did not mislead you in that compartment, he shouldn't raise anything now that you haven't already heard from him. But let him talk, and then use your features and benefits to convince him that you can solve the problem.

Once John says he is in agreement, 100 percent, you can then tackle the second and the third pains in the same fashion.

The Thermometer Technique

Before you proceed with any more pain, however, use the Thermometer technique, which helps you measure the degree to which your prospect has been sold. Here's how it works:

"John, we've covered a lot of ground so far, and there's still more to show you, but on a 0-to-10 scale, 0 meaning you have no interest in my service and 10 meaning you have already decided to buy my service, where are you?"

If he says he's a 10, there is no need to finish your presentation. Pains 4 and 5 are irrelevant. The deal is done!

If the prospect is less than a 6, you've got a problem. In our present scenario, John already has said "yes" to you three times. He's agreed with you 100 percent three times. So why is he less than a 6? Did you push too fast? Did you assume he was 100 percent when he wasn't? To find out what went wrong, ask him!

"John, based on what you've told me so far, I don't understand why you say you're a 4. Can you help me understand that?"

Whatever John says will reveal deeper pain, new pain, or pain that your Fulfillment step hasn't alleviated. Be patient. Listen. And begin the process again.

Most of the time, at this stage of Fulfillment, your prospect will be higher than 6. In that event, you say:

"John, what do you need to see to get to 10?"

And then, whatever he has to see is what you show him—nothing more and nothing less. After you've shown him what he's asked for, check his temperature again:

"John, on that 0-to-10 scale, where are you now?"

You can bet he'll be moving upward, and eventually he'll arrive at a 10. Now, this is important. When your prospect arrives at 10, don't use a worn-out traditional close like "Want me to write it up?" Instead, simply ask this question:

"What would you like me to do now?"

See what you just did? You placed the pressure where it belongs—on the prospect. Let the prospect tell you what to do. Let the prospect close the sale. That way, the prospect remains in control, and the prospect can never accuse you of forcing the sale.

Now that's exciting, don't you agree?

The Money Barrier

There's one other problem that frequently occurs in the Fulfillment step. It's money! Sometimes your prospect won't be able to buy what you're offering, even though that wasn't clear in the Budget step. If you suspect that's the case, for whatever reason, complete your presentation, seek the prospect's agreement that your product or service can provide the necessary solutions, but then, instead of using the Thermometer technique, try this approach:

"John, earlier we both agreed that your budget for this service is $5,000. If I remember correctly, you said you have $2,500 of this money available now—it's in your checking account—and you could charge another $2,500 on your credit card, your Visa, I believe you told me. Now, all of your problems can be solved with Service X, which requires an investment of $4,700, or, if you can live with a couple of the problems you're trying to solve, you could purchase Service Y, which requires an investment of $3,500. Do you have any feelings as to which one or more of the benefits that you want could be eliminated, . . . or shall we get the job done first class and choose Service X?

If John chooses X or Y, the Fulfillment step is over!

SANDLER SELLING TIP

There are no bad prospects, only bad salespeople. If you get this far along in the process, and you somehow end up not getting the deal, rest assured that you missed something along the way. Don't be a victim. Don't rationalize what happened. Don't blame the lost sale on a prospect's personality or actions. Don't blame your team. Don't blame your presentation software or your website. Don't allow yourself to get caught up in the "that-guy-wouldn't-buy-from-anyone" syndrome, either. Do assume full accountability. Whatever is happening in your relationship with a prospect or customer, whether it's looking like success or looking like failure, is your responsibility. You can never control what happens on the other side. All you can control is your own attitude, behavior, and techniques.   —DHM

Congratulations! You're on your way to the bank. But not so fast. There's still one more compartment to seal up before this sale is completed.

15

DON'T LET BUYER'S REMORSE SINK YOUR SALE

The sale is closed when you get the

order, collect the check, take it to

the bank, and the check clears!

—DAVID H. SANDLER

A t this point in professional selling, nothing ever feels better than the way you feel right now! You found a suspect, turned him into a prospect, expertly led him through the compartments of the Sandler Submarine, and now you're sitting in front of your new customer with your order in hand. It just doesn't get any better than this for those of us in the sales profession, does it?

So what happens next?

If you've been trained traditionally, you've been taught that your next move is to shut up and run. Traditional sales trainers have been teaching for years that once you get the order, you don't say another word. You could talk your new customer right out of the sale! The deal is done. Don't chance saying something that will sink the sale. Take your contract, pack up your belongings, and get out of there. And don't forget to shake your new customer 's hand on your way out the door.

What's the hurry?

Well, the traditional salesperson's dog-and-pony show, which was punctuated with enthusiastic antics that released tension and distracted the prospect, most likely included some sort of slam-dunk close. Therefore, the traditional salesperson has to move fast. Her prospect is about to regain his senses, and when he does, he's likely to cancel the sale. By getting out of the way as quickly as possible, the traditionalist figures that once she's out of sight, she's out of mind. Her new customer will move on to the next project on his desk and forget about the contract he just signed. Meanwhile, the traditionalist returns to her office and processes the order. "Got another one," she announces proudly to everyone at the office.

Unfortunately, the traditional salesperson underestimates Buyer's Remorse, a disease that frequently sinks the best of sales. Sooner or later, the prospect begins to second-guess what he just signed. Prospects who feel they were manipulated in any way are almost certain to cancel the order and kill the sale. Other prospects will back out simply because they weren't convinced by the sales presentation. And just as the traditional salesperson is about to scoot out to the bank to deposit the customer's check, she gets a telephone call. She can't believe it as she listens to her new customer say, "Hold up on that order. There's a new wrinkle that I've got to solve first. Call me in a few weeks."

While nothing ever feels better to a salesperson than watching a prospect sign a sales agreement, nothing feels worse than losing the sale before the ink is dry! You want to avoid going back to your office with a signed contract only to find a voice mail message or an email that says your new customer has changed his mind.

Express Your Feelings Through Third-Party Stories

Have you ever walked away from a sales call feeling uncomfortable, even though you had closed the sale? Your new client said yes, but you sensed something was wrong, yet you were afraid to say it out loud. Later, you probably lost the sale. Whatever was making you feel uncomfortable was probably nagging at your client too. Once you were gone, Buyer's Remorse took over, and the sale was sunk.

Next time you're at a sales call and feeling uncomfortable, why not just raise the issue? Take a stab at that uncomfortable feeling while you still have the opportunity to save the order.

If you find it awkward to express yourself in these situations, try using a third-party story. For example, suppose your prospect pressured you over the price of your product but still said "yes" to your offer. Rather than defending your position, you should tell your prospect how you feel. Here's an easy way to do it:

"George, just last week when I was working with a client, I really felt uncomfortable. What had happened was that after agreeing to the sale, and after I went to my home office with the order, the client changed the rules on me. He canceled the order. It really made me feel uncomfortable. If I go to my home office and get this price for you, that won't happen with us, will it, George?"

Try it, and see if it doesn't work!

SANDLER SELLING TIP

Don't buy back tomorrow the product or service you sold today. You got a YES! That's great. Instead of rushing to the office to process the order before the prospect changes his mind, give the person the chance to back out, while the two of you are talking, before you seal the deal. Validate that the customer really is okay with your path forward and will not bring any deal-changing issues up again unless you are part of the conversation.

This is the step that brand-new Sandler students are most likely to avoid implementing. The salesperson who skips the Post-Sell, however, is far more likely to receive a curt, brief email from the customer he just closed informing him that "something has come up." That "something" usually delays, postpones, or otherwise derails the sale. If you don't want to get that kind of email message—and who does?—complete this compartment of the Sandler Submarine. When you give people the opportunity to change their mind and talk it through with you one more time after they've said yes, they review and reflect, and they cement their commitment to move forward. They are then *less* likely to change their mind about buying from you.

The reality is, everyone gets Buyer's Remorse. The Sandler difference is that we get our customers to agree to have it while they're talking to us.   —DHM

The Post-Sell compartment of the Sandler Submarine is designed to help you avoid the effects of Buyer's Remorse. You can't stop Buyer's Remorse because it's a natural phenomenon. Almost everyone who buys something of consequence experiences Buyer's Remorse. However, you can almost always stop Buyer's Remorse from reaching into your pocket and canceling a sales agreement.

If you used the techniques that I've described so far in this book to lead your prospect to sign your sales agreement, you've already begun to protect yourself from Buyer's Remorse. Look what happened as you used the Sandler Selling System:

> Your prospect felt in control throughout the selling cycle, from start to finish.
> The prospect decided to buy or not to buy. There was never *any* pressure.
> The prospect owns the decision.
> And therefore, the prospect has no need to escape.

Is the prospect still likely to be afflicted by Buyer's Remorse? Absolutely. But now there's something you can do to lock up the sale for good. *Give your new customer a little dose of Buyer's Remorse even while you're still on the scene!* If there's a crack in the sale, check for it now while you still have an opportunity to patch it up on the spot.

Here's what you do:

1. Close the sale. Do all the things you need to do to officially take the order. Get the agreement signed. Give the customer a copy. Fill out the purchase order or pick up the check. Finalize the delivery date. Clear away all the details.

2. Thank your customer for the order. "Steve, I appreciate your business, and I want you to know that everything we discussed will be handled just as I said. I'll get right on it." Shake hands.

3. Deliberately bring up a mutually agreed-upon compromise that occurred during the selling cycle. *Begin by saying this:*

"Before I go, Steve, there's something that's left me a little uncomfortable about one of the items we agreed upon during our conversation."

Now, explain the compromise. For example:

"You originally wanted an XYZ computer configuration, and after some discussion you agreed that a combination of XYZ and ABC configurations would make more sense, because of the many different end users in your network. . . ."

Finish by saying:

"I bring this up, Steve, because I don't want to leave today and then have you call me at a later date and cancel the order because of it. You wouldn't cancel because of the change we agreed upon, would you, Steve?"

It doesn't make any difference which compromise you recall. What's important is that you give your prospect an opportunity to back out while you're still in the room. Your prospect will almost always agree to the compromise. But if for some reason your prospect is uncomfortable, now's the time to find out. You can still fix it!

Here's another way to use the Post-Sell step:

Hand Steve the signed agreement and ask, "Now, Steve, do you know what this is?"

Steve will say, "Sure, it's the agreement I just signed with you."

And you say: "Not only is it our agreement, Steve, but it's also the solutions to your [Pain 1, Pain 2, Pain 3]. If there are any doubts about moving forward, Steve, let's discuss them now. [Pause] If not, you're telling me you're moving forward, and I won't receive a message from you tomorrow telling me you've changed your mind. Is that fair?"

> Even if the prospect suffers some Buyer's Remorse after you're out of sight, the fact that you gave the prospect the opportunity to back out will play a large part in the prospect's decision not to cancel the order.

Even if the prospect suffers some Buyer's Remorse after you're out of sight, the fact that you gave the prospect the opportunity to back out will play a large part in the prospect's decision not to cancel the order. When Buyer's Remorse strikes the prospect, your Post-Sell step won't be forgotten.

"Hmmm. I wonder if I made the right decision," thinks the prospect during a fit of Buyer's Remorse. "Should I call Jerry back in here and put off the decision for a few more weeks? Well, I already said I wouldn't cancel. And besides, the company needs the new system now. I said I'd move forward, and I'm going to."

The sale is sealed. You've done everything you've been trained to do.

Practice, Practice, Practice

I've taught you the steps of a new and effective sales system, one that's being used by thousands of people in the United States today. You've learned to seal off each compartment of the Sandler Submarine. Use the techniques you've learned in this book, and you can keep your sales career afloat. No one can sink your sales any longer. No one but you!

Remember: You can't teach a kid to ride a bike at a seminar! It takes practice. You've got to try it and fall down, get up and do it again, and repeat the process over and over again. And then suddenly, the system will work, and you'll *own* it forever. In fact, eventually as you use this system, you'll forget that you read about it in this book. That's when the system belongs to you!

To hurry up the process of owning this system, practice it as often as you can. I recommend that you practice with others. Reinforcement training with a group is an exciting way to hone your selling skills. In communities across the United States, groups of professionals meet weekly to practice the Sandler Selling System. For information about a group in your area, please visit www.sandler.com.

Now the only rule to remember is a simple one: *The sale is closed when you get the order, collect the check, take it to the bank, and it clears!*

SANDLER SELLING TIP

Sandler Enterprise Selling. There are special challenges to selling to a prospect who operates in an environment where there are multiple silos, multiple constituencies, and multiple decision makers. In a traditional sale—a sale that closes in a relatively short period of time and has a straightforward decision-making process—the proven model for success is the Sandler Submarine. As you've seen, that model begins with Bonding and Rapport and ends with the Post-Sell. But in more complex selling situations, many additional variables enter the picture.

With these accounts, selling cycles are extended; buyer networks are wide and diverse. The decision process involves people from multiple teams. In more strategic pursuits, our competition tends to be far more sophisticated, and knowledge about the buying organization itself becomes a much more important asset. Team selling is a critical survival skill in this environment. The rewards here are greater, but the risks are greater too. The landscape here can change quickly. When you sell in this arena, it's imperative that you have a clear process that ensures that you are targeting the deals you are most likely to win, and that you continue to make good, strategically sound decisions about whether to continue or exit a particular pursuit. This is the world of enterprise accounts.

With enterprise accounts, lots of important things must happen *before* Bonding and Rapport . . . and *after* the Post-Sell. In between, there are plenty of moving parts that can make executing the various compartments of the Submarine a big challenge. The goal of serving clients and expanding relationships over time becomes a major issue . . . and a game-changing opportunity.

Sandler Enterprise Selling (SES) is a flexible program that incorporates all the elements of the Sandler Submarine. It addresses the special requirements of sales teams who sell into complex accounts. Visit us at www.sandler.com/enterpriseselling or call 410-559-2003 for information on SES.   —DHM

16

GETTING THE ANGLE ON SUCCESS

Techniques are important, but salespeople
who learn to deliver their techniques
with the appropriate attitude and
behavior get to the bank most often.

—DAVID H. SANDLER

I n the first chapter of this book, I told you how you can conquer professional selling.

"You need to learn a system," I wrote. "You need to master techniques, but not traditional sales techniques. You need to be nurtured, and supported, not for a day or two but for months, if not years."

Throughout the balance of this book, I explained the Sandler Selling System, a nontraditional approach to professional selling currently used by thousands of successful practitioners.

I also demonstrated the techniques that we've created at our company. The proper use of these techniques makes the Sandler Selling System effective and fun!

Most important of all, the techniques will get you to the bank more often.

Furthermore, I urged you to practice the techniques. I suggested that you seek out support programs. Once you master the techniques, you will gain the upper hand in the selling dance that always occurs when salesperson meets prospect.

However, I also said in that first chapter, "Selling professionally requires modification of your behavior and the altering of preconceived ideas that have been ingrained in the minds of both salespeople and prospects for centuries." Therefore, there's still one more compartment to the system. If you're committed to mastering the Sandler Selling System, the information in this final chapter will propel your learning curve and help you *own* the system. After that, I promise you that you can achieve the success you want as a sales professional.

Nine Reasons to Set Goals

Goal setting:

1. Can be used to improve your I (identity).
2. Can be used to improve your R (role).
3. Makes you aware of your strengths (so you're better prepared to overcome obstacles and provide solutions to problems).
4. Points out your weaknesses (so you can begin setting new goals to improve on your weaknesses and turn them into strengths).
5. Helps you identify successes that will motivate you toward new goals.
6. Gives you a track to run on.
7. Forces you to set priorities that establish direction for your pursuits.
8. Separates reality from wishful thinking and eliminates daydreaming.
9. Makes you responsible for your own life because it forces you to define and establish your value system.

> Technique training alone will not make a successful salesperson.

Let me ask you a question: How effective are you in an actual buyer-seller situation?

Having read this book, you might say that with the techniques you've just learned, you are going to be more effective in future buyer-seller situations than you've ever been before. I would agree, at least for the short term. However, technique training alone will not make a successful salesperson. Techniques are important, but salespeople who learn to deliver their techniques with the appropriate *attitude* and *behavior* get to the bank most often.

Motivation Isn't a Set of Power Phrases

When traditional sales trainers talk about motivation, they usually do a lot of shouting and jumping. They're like cheerleaders with a big capital M on their sweaters, and their mission is to get everyone in their audience excited by shouting one-liners and power phrases.

Of course, it doesn't work. The audience is pumped up for a day or two, but then it's back to business as usual. The excitement is gone. And motivation never existed.

Motivation is not some mystical pump-up program.

Motivation is the ability to see in the present a projection of the future that you want for yourself; to put into motion the plan for its achievement; to be aware of the price required to achieve your goals; and then to move steadily toward these goals on a day-to-day basis.

All the one-liners and power phrases known to humanity and wrapped up in a positive mental attitude won't get you past the first coffee shop unless you know where you're going. Only motivation will do that.

Do you want to get to the top of the sales profession? Then I encourage you to work on each of these three elements: attitude, behavior, and technique. When you're proficient in these three areas, selling becomes everything you ever dreamed it could be.

Take a look at Figure 16.1, which includes a series of triangles. You'll notice that the Success triangle is connected to the three triangles of Attitude, Behavior, and Technique. You might say, in fact, that Success is dependent upon Attitude, Behavior, and Technique and that each of those triangles is dependent upon each other, as well as success. Convenient, huh?

Figure 16.1 *The Success Triangle*

Actually, the relationship of these triangles clearly depicts what we've learned about successful selling at our company. We've tested thousands of salespeople through the years and measured their productivity against their scores in each of the triangles. (Please visit us at www.sandler.com/certification for more information about our testing and certification procedures.)

Perhaps the illustration of the triangles in Figure 16.1 will help you understand why technique training alone won't allow you to conquer the sales profession. As you can see, Technique is only one leg of the tripod that supports success. Look closely and you'll see that you've already learned about the issues and skills that affect the Technique triangle. Earlier in this book you read about the tactics of the Dummy Curve, the Reverse, and the Negative Reverse Sell. You learned the strategies for qualifying prospects, presenting information, and closing a sale. You read about the issues related to personal presence.

All of the issues and skills are interconnected, as you can see by the triangles. Failure to perform in any one triangle will destroy the effectiveness of the Technique triangle. The consequence? Overall failure, or at least a less-than-successful outcome.

At the same time, perfection with the Technique triangle will not guarantee overall success in professional selling unless there's equal emphasis exerted in the Behavior and Attitude triangles.

Courage Is an Action Word

Courage is not about taking a risk, and it's not about undertaking new ventures.

Courage is all about taking action. Courage requires discipline, vitality, and guts to face those tasks in your profession that make you feel uncomfortable.

Accepting a no isn't an act of courage, unless a no bothers you. Asking for money when it pains you to do so is an act of courage. It's not an act of courage to seek out the decision maker if seeking out the decision maker doesn't bother you. It's an act of courage to seek out the decision maker when it pains you to do so.

It's easy to single out the superstars in professional selling, place them on pedestals, and pay homage to their deeds when their deeds are so fearful to us. Do these superstars draw upon some unknown courage that the rest of us know nothing about? Probably not. Through past experiences, knowledge, and pain, the superstars found courage in the past and today they perform without it.

Courage belongs to every salesperson who faces an inner fear. In your darkest moments, sitting on the edge of your bed at night, making the day-to-day decision to remain in professional selling, looking for the strength to face tomorrow, and deciding to deal with your fears . . . that takes courage.

What a shame that we are sometimes so overwhelmed by our fears that we can't see that our finest characteristic is about to take us to new heights . . . and its name is courage.

The synergy of the triangles creates success. All of the pieces must be accounted for by the super salesperson. One piece may demand more time than another. One issue or skill may be easier to perfect than another. But the super salesperson learns that all of the pieces are necessary to build and support a rewarding career in professional selling.

If selling were a mechanical process, then we could focus only on technique training. In that case, what you've read up to this final chapter would be enough information to help you succeed in sales. However, you'd have many more times the competition—good competition too—because techniques are easy to learn. Anyone who could master the Reverse, the Dummy Curve, the Negative Reverse Sell, and other techniques could become successful at selling.

But that's not the way it works because selling is more conceptual than it is mechanical. Style is more effective than substance in selling, and therefore, technique without comprehension yields only short-term gains. Based on our company's experiences, we know that technique and personality work together to form super salespeople. It's important that you learn to incorporate the techniques of the Sandler Selling System within your own personality. The discussion surrounding the Attitude and Behavior triangles sheds more light on this subject.

Be a Self-Starter

A high-powered sports car has a tremendous amount of potential energy, but it cannot leave the starting gate until someone turns on its ignition.

The powerful engines of a wide-bodied jet cannot lift the plane an inch off the ground without someone first activating its controls.

A locomotive under power can smash through a brick wall 10 feet thick! But it can't move until someone fires up the engine.

Machines cannot turn themselves on. But people can!

Too many people sit around waiting to be motivated—as if some chemical reaction can propel them into action. Self-starters know better. They act on their goals, and they know that the motivation they need is built into the goals.

If you're not feeling "up to it," no amount of concentration, wishful thinking, or smokescreen planning will get you moving. Remember Newton's law? Things in motion tend to stay in motion; things at rest remain at rest. The more you think about becoming motivated, the better the chances that you won't.

> Machines cannot turn themselves on. But people can!

Self-starters know there's never a "right" time to get started. Regardless of how they feel at any given moment, how they feel in the next moment is determined by the actions they take.

If you set worthwhile goals, and you've developed a plan of action, you can set your plan into action any time of day or night simply by acting. It's how you act that determines how you feel; how you feel does not determine how you act.

Don't lose precious time by waiting for the "right" time. Become a self-starter!

How Important Is Attitude?

Attitude is on top of the Success triangle because attitude dominates all of the other functions of success. It's a safe bet that your performance is consistent with the way you view yourself conceptually. Your mindset, or your outlook, controls your behavior, your use of techniques, your actions, tactics, strategies—*everything* that determines failure or success in your life. You take your outlook with you no matter where you go in life. If, for example, you're one of the top producers in your company and you resign tomorrow, wherever you go you're going to reach the top again. You'll get the same training as your peers, and you'll sell the same product or service, and work from the same pool of leads, but you'll outperform most of the others simply because of your attitude. It's so predictable that it's frightening! Attitude determines results, good or bad.

Attitude is never nonexistent. It's not like an illness that comes and goes. It's always present. Even in our sleep, attitude can be reflected in our dreams. However, it's when we awake in the morning that attitude shifts into gear and begins to control the rest of the day.

What Motivates You?

Select a short-term (30-day) income or sales goal that far exceeds anything you've accomplished in the past and write the goal on a three-by-five card.

Next, looking at the goal you set for yourself, note on the card the percentage chance you give yourself for achieving this goal. In other words, is there a 10 percent chance you'll achieve it, or a 90 percent chance? (Don't fool yourself. There's no need to blue-sky this decision. My experience is that a truthful percentage is in the 10 to 25 percent range.)

There are two things I can now tell you about your goal:

1. The goal you set for yourself is attainable.
2. You have a 100 percent chance of achieving it.

Here's the scenario:

You've just been informed that a terrorist group has kidnapped someone very dear to you—your spouse, a parent, or one of your children. The terrorists have informed you that your only chance of seeing your loved one again is to achieve the short-term goal you described on the three-by-five card.

You've got 30 days. Now, what will you do?

Will you end your workday at five o'clock?
Will you seek out the decision makers?

Will you accept "I want to think it over" for an answer?
Will you need motivational crutches?
Will you ask for pain?
Will you establish Up-Front Contracts?
Will you sleep nights?
Will you accomplish your goal?

There's no doubt about it, you'll do whatever it takes to achieve your goal in that scenario.

So what does this exercise tell you? Only that you have always had the ability to achieve your goals. But until now, the price wasn't right!

You have the ability to do the job. What you don't have is the motivation to do the job to the best of your ability.

The only question that remains is simply this: *What motivates you?*

Set Yourself Up for a Victory

Can you remember your first thought when you woke up this morning? Even if you can't remember it, I'm going to assume that most of you did not wake up before dawn and proclaim to the bedroom: "It's another great day to enter the winner's circle, and I'm going to begin by taking a cold shower!" Sounds a bit too enthusiastic for a predawn hour, doesn't it?

One of our company's top-producing franchisees—who sells more than a million dollars of products and services every year—does, in fact, get up before dawn every day to take a cold shower. Why? He says he does it because a cold shower wakes him up! However, he also says the cold shower is symbolic of winning. He could "wimp out," he explains, and take a comfortable, hot shower, or he could immediately jump into the winner's circle by taking a cold shower.

And why is that important?

Because he understands that just to *feel* he's winning is motivation enough to go on and win!

That's exciting! We don't have to win to win. We simply have to *feel* like we're winning . . . the feeling will give us the motivation to go on and win.

If you want to influence your own positive attitude, find ways to set yourself up to win. Day by day, moment by moment, look for opportunities to win, even if they are little victories. If a cold shower before dawn registers as a victory for you, then take one! Get into the habit of feeling like you are winning. Separate your I from your R and protect your attitude.

You Can Change a Bad Attitude

Do you have to begin your day with a cold shower to become a super salesperson? Of course not. But to begin your day without the feeling that you're ready to win, or that you're going to win, is enough to sabotage the rest of your day. How many people get out of bed in the morning and say something like this: "Ugh, another day, another dollar. Here I go off to work again." With that kind of attitude, is it any wonder that the day turns out to be less than spectacular?

It's Time to Live a Little!

Here's an exercise that will help you get motivated. I call it simply the Lifeline:

1. Draw a horizontal line at the top of a piece of paper.
2. Write the letter B at the left edge of the line and the letter D at the right edge of the line. So far, your Lifeline should look like this:

B   D

3. Above the B, write the year of your birth.
4. This next assignment is a bit unusual, but take your time and follow through, please. Above the D, write the year of your death. There's no way to know the year, of course, but take a guess. Perhaps you've thought about the age at which you'd like to die. Go ahead; note the year right above the D.
5. Now, find your present age on the Lifeline, and mark it with a P. The P should be placed in relation to the other letters. For example,

if you plan to live to be 100 and you are now 50, you'd place the letter P in the exact center of the line. Your Lifeline would look like this:

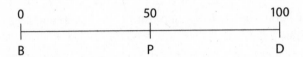

6. Place an R on your Lifeline to indicate your retirement age. Retirement doesn't necessarily mean you'll stop working. It means you could stop working at that age if you wanted to. So if you're 50 years old planning to live to be 100, but you'll retire at 75, you'd place the R exactly three-fourths of the way across the line. Now your Lifeline would look like this:

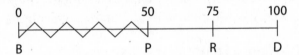

7. Draw a wavy line from B through P. That's the past. Those years now represent your experience. The past is over.

Now, begin the rest of your life, from P to D. There's a worn-out one-liner that says: "Today is the first day of the rest of your life." Now that you've drawn your Lifeline, that saying has never been more true for you.

By the way, whatever year you wrote above the D, erase it. Add another 10 years. It's your choice, so live a little!

After drawing your Lifeline, I suggest you take inventory of where you are right now. On a blank sheet of paper, set up columns with the following headings: Work, Family, Spiritual, Financial, Self-Personal, Health, Social, and Education. Under each heading write a brief statement of your present situation.

Now, take a second sheet of paper, list the same headings and columns, and write what you would like to accomplish between the P and R on your Lifeline. From the present until you retire, what do you want to accomplish under Work, Family, Spiritual, Financial, and so forth?

Use a third sheet of paper with the same headings and columns, and write what you would like to accomplish between R and D in your Lifeline.

Finally, for the next three days concentrate on the information you wrote under each of the headings. Think about the information. Do you want to eliminate certain items? Do you want to add others? Continue this editing process until you're satisfied with your goals.

Then, get on with living your life!

The good thing about a bad attitude is that you can change it. In fact, your attitude fluctuates. It changes from day to day, from moment to moment. You're in control of the fluctuations, but it's so easy to allow a given situation to wrestle the control from you. For example, you start out the day with a winning attitude. You arrive at work feeling rested, energetic, and enthusiastic. You grab the telephone and begin making cold calls. And what happens? The first three or four negative calls don't bother you much. Your attitude dissolves any negativity. But after the tenth negative call, the wind has been knocked out of your positive attitude. Suddenly, on a scale of 0 to 10, you're hanging on the bottom rung. You spend the rest of your morning trying to get your attitude back up to 10, but it's about all you can do just to pick up the phone.

What really happened? You let emotion take control of your attitude. When a single event, or a combination of related events, such as negative phone calls, affects your attitude, you've surrendered to your emotion. And as long as that emotion dominates your thought process, your attitude remains sour, and it's nearly impossible to win. "What's the use?" you say to yourself. "I've made 35 phone calls, but it's hopeless." The emotion that accompanies that thought is called *despair*, or *resignation*. It's the opposite of feeling that winning is possible. And in that frame of mind, it's a struggle to think positively or to adjust your attitude.

> When a single event, or a combination of related events, such as negative phone calls, affects your attitude, you've surrendered to your emotion.

The Self-Image Triangle

Attitude is an outcome of your self-image. When your self-image is strong, negativity takes less of a toll on your attitude. Therefore, it's important to believe in yourself. How you feel about yourself on any given day is going to determine your attitude. In the illustration of triangles in Figure 16.2, you'll notice that You sits just above the top point of the Attitude triangle, and that You is itself part of the triangle composed of Spirit, Mind, and Body.

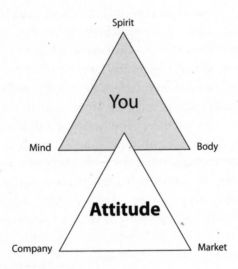

Figure 16.2 *The Self-Image Triangle*

The You triangle is called the Self-Image triangle. It is your I (identity), and when it's strong, negative events simply roll off your back. If you get wiped out by a telephone call, you'll simply pick up the phone and make another call. When you understand that your I and your R (role) are not interdependent, it's much easier to cultivate a positive attitude.

Quite often, salespeople think they're slacking in performance because they don't set goals, or they don't work their plan, or they don't execute their techniques effectively in front of a prospect. So they attend seminars and workshops with the hope that they can improve their performance. And what happens? Usually not much. Performance improves for a week or two, if that, and then it's back to the same old pathetic story. Only now, the attitude is even worse! And all the while, the effort was expended on the wrong end of the problem!

Try the Birdcage Challenge!

Let's say I give you a birdcage, and you take it home and hang it in the kitchen where it's visible. There's just one catch: you've got to keep a bird out of the cage for 30 days or you lose the challenge. And there's just one rule: you can't tell anyone you want to keep the cage empty!

Here's what's going to happen.

Your family members will see the birdcage, but they'll be hesitant to ask you why it's in the kitchen. They'll probably decide to take a wait-and-see position for a few days.

However, one of your neighbors will drop by to visit, see the cage, and ask you, "Where's the bird?"

You'll reply, "Don't have a bird." The neighbor will give you a strange look but drop the subject.

Several more neighbors will visit, and you'll go through a similar routine. You'll decide to cover the cage, but then a neighbor will ask, "Bird sleeping?"

You'll reply, "Don't have a bird."

The neighbor will ask, "Why would you put a cover on a cage that doesn't have a bird in it?"

You'll shrug and the neighbor will move on. Remember, you can't tell anyone you want to keep the cage empty!

About three weeks into the challenge, you'll think you've got it made. No one's asking you about your missing bird anymore, and you're now counting the days to your victory.

But what you don't know is that your family has called a private meeting behind your back. "Looks like Dad wants a bird," they agree. "What do you think? Yep! Let's go to the pet store and get him one."

That evening, you return home, and there it is, a bird in your cage!

Now, what's the moral of this story?

It's very simple: Decide what you want (that's the bird), build a plan (that's the cage), and you can bet on the outcome (the goal). The minute you set up your "cage" you've already achieved your goal. It's just a matter of time until you collect.

More often than not, low self-esteem is the real problem behind an undesirable attitude. Therefore, for many people, the quickest way to achieve success is to work on the You triangle.

Is that what you need to improve your attitude?

Take a moment and assess the condition of your spirit, mind, and body. If any one area needs work, focus on it. That could be the missing element that's affecting your attitude.

At the left point of the Attitude triangle, you'll find Company, and at the right point, there's Market. These two issues also affect your attitude. It's important to like your company and the marketplace in which you sell. While you could be spiritually, mentally, and physically healthy, if you're unhappy about your coworkers, or you don't like the products you sell, or you don't believe in your marketplace, your attitude will suffer. It may be positive one day and negative the next, and you will constantly struggle to control the fluctuations.

It's important to point out that people who score high in the You triangle tend to have fewer problems in the Company or Market triangles. People with a low self-image tend to externalize their problems. Rather than looking inward for a solution, they choose to blame the company, the product, or the economic conditions of the marketplace. People with a high self-image will turn inward and ask what they can do to change the circumstances. Nonetheless, to become a peak performer in professional selling you must condition yourself in all of these areas.

How Important Is Behavior?

Focus now on the left corner of the Success triangle, and you'll find Behavior in a triangle consisting of Actions, Plans, and Goals. Behavior is all about the way you spend your time. (Review the A/B Journal in Chapter 4.) Some people are more productive than others because they behave differently than others. Anyone who has read a book about selling or attended a seminar has heard about the importance of behavior, and especially about goal setting. (Throughout this chapter, you'll find numerous exercises that are designed to help you improve the behavior-related triangles.)

The relationship of your Behavior triangle to your Attitude triangle explains your level of commitment. People who score low in the

Attitude triangle are likely to also score low in the Behavior triangle. These are the people who have little *commitment,* and that's why success escapes them.

When we find someone who scores low in both the Attitude and Behavior triangles, we suggest they work first on behavior. If they'll commit to reaching certain goals—through better planning and action—they'll improve their attitude in a short period of time even without working on their attitude. *People who act committed feel better about themselves.* At our company, we say, "It's not how you feel that determines how you act. It's how you act that determines how you feel."

SANDLER SELLING TIP

The Success triangle has three points, not one. For most of us, it's pretty easy to work on the Technique point of the Success triangle. That's the part of the triangle focused on things like "What do I say to the prospect?"

Yet what keeps top sales performers effective over the long term isn't the "What do I say?" point of the triangle. They've got that down. It's the Attitude component—"*Why* am I saying this?"—and the Behavior component, the daily accountabilities that turn into "muscle memory." Those are the elements that tend to make the biggest difference over time in terms of individual sales production.

Did you know that, statistically, sales go through the roof right after the holidays for gym memberships? These places actually plan for most of their customers *not* to show up a month or two after they make their New Year's resolutions. Management knows that most people won't follow through, and they staff accordingly. Why is that? And even more important, how is it that the people who operate gyms have figured out what most professional salespeople haven't?

Like the vast majority of the folks who show up at the gym in January, most salespeople and organizations work on only one part of the triangle. They work on the "what to do," but rarely do they work on the "why to do it" and the daily accountabilities. In fact, most salespeople have got the "what" down to an art form. High performers, on the other hand, work consistently on all three elements of the triangle.   —DHM

Trap Yourself into Achieving Your Goals

Everyone, sooner or later, consciously or not, sets a goal. But unfortunately, most people never achieve their goals, even simple goals. Some people just don't know how. Others try, but they get distracted by all the other things going on about them.

But now, I'm going to introduce you to a "sure thing" for achieving goals. Here's a trap that will trick you into achieving first a little goal, and then larger goals. Eventually, you'll become an expert at setting and achieving your goals. Here's how it works:

Think of something minor that you've been meaning to accomplish for weeks or months, or maybe even years. Be sure it's minor. It could be related to your business, but it might involve a project at home. Some examples are repairing the screen door, fixing a leaky faucet, beginning to read a novel, grooming the dog, or cleaning out the refrigerator. Nothing major.

Now, get a piece of paper about the size of a three-by-five card. Whatever it is you've been talking about doing for so long, write it on the paper. For example: "Fix leaky faucet in the bathroom."

Then, on the back side of the paper write the following: "I promise that by [write in the date—make it 30 days from today's date] I will fix the leaky faucet in the bathroom." Sign the paper. And fold it to about the size of a penny.

Put that piece of paper in your pocket, and for the next 30 days don't let it get away from you. If you carry change in your pocket, keep the piece of paper with your change. For the next several days, whenever you empty your pocket, unfold that piece of paper and read it to yourself. After several days, you won't have to unfold the paper and read it anymore, but when you notice the paper, you have to mentally repeat the goal to yourself. "I promise that by [date] I will fix the leaky faucet in the bathroom."

I promise you that goal will be fulfilled by the date on the piece of paper. You can fight against it, and it won't make any difference. The goal is done. You'll get it done, and you'll do it in a hurry.

When you finish that little goal, try another one. And continue repeating the exercise. You will eventually realize that whatever you commit to paper and then think about repeatedly actually gets done.

Make your next goal a little bigger. Soon you'll need a larger piece of paper—and eventually a notebook—to keep track of your goals!

Commitment helps you survive the test of adversity. If adversity strikes when your commitment is low or nonexistent, fear, doubt, and worry will force you to give up. That's why it's so important to work on your Behavior triangle.

The easiest way to improve your behavior is to set goals. When you set a goal, you formulate a working plan, and you get results when you take action. It's a good idea to set simple goals at first, or goals that you can quickly achieve. *Get into the habit of winning.* The sooner you do, the sooner you'll affect your attitude.

SANDLER SELLING TIP

Winners will always be in demand. Times change and technologies change, but goal-oriented salespeople who harness the combined power of behavior, attitude, and technique will never go out of style, and the sales profession itself will never go the way of the dinosaur. —DHM

Ultimately, commitment is what counts. Are you willing to commit to be successful? If you are, and you apply the appropriate degree of commitment, success is yours. The combination of behavior, attitude, and technique will provide any level of success you desire. You need nothing more, or less. Apply your energies to each of these triangles, and you will own the Sandler Selling System.

One final word: Enjoy your frequent trips to the bank!

A

CASE STUDIES

Rohrer's: "Three Generations of Sandler!"

Company Description

Rohrer's One Hour Heating & Air Conditioning is the leading heating, ventilation, and air-conditioning (HVAC) service provider in the Lancaster, Pennsylvania, area.

Accolades

The company currently maintains a rating of five out of five stars from Businessfinder.Pennlive.com, with over 100 company-specific consumer reviews posted.

Key Challenges

Back in 1990, owner Larry Rohrer's goal was both simple and far-reaching. He wanted to give his people an enduring competitive advantage that few, if any, local HVAC competitors would be likely to offer. He asked Sandler Training to develop and reinforce a comprehensive suite of tools that would allow his people to accomplish the following:

- Increase sales performance
- Deliver superior customer service
- Function effectively as a cohesive team

As Rohrer told us, he wanted to work with someone who understood that **"everyone in the organization can and does sell."**

Sandler Solution

We made an ongoing commitment to train and reinforce the Sandler principles over time. This commitment extended not just to the sales team but also to **everyone** in the organization, over a continuous period of **23 years ... and counting.**

Company Website

http://www.onehourairhelp.com/

Business Challenge

When we first met Rohrer HVAC in 1990, it was a 31-year-old company with an ambitious plan. Owner Larry Rohrer was committed not only to expanding sales revenue but also to **creating an overall customer experience that made it easy for salespeople to sell on something other than price.**

Rohrer's success story is a powerful one because the company's goals were always focused on delivering high value to customers by means of a sales-driven internal culture. Larry Rohrer told us that he didn't just want himself and his one salesperson (at the time) to follow the Sandler principles. He wanted everyone in the organization to learn the principles and to operate in accordance with them both internally and externally. He wanted the principles to be taught and reinforced constantly, up and down the organization.

We have honored that commitment for nearly a quarter of a century, and we have been privileged to continue our work with the Rohrer family even after Larry retired and ownership of the company passed to a second generation. Larry's son Scott Rohrer is now co-owner of the firm, with Matt Buckwalter. Both are Sandler alumni, as are *all* of the organization's employees: every customer care associate, every technician, and of course, every salesperson.

Buckwalter, who came on board as a salesperson with the company in 2000, had no sales experience or training whatsoever before being trained in the Sandler Selling System. He reports that it took him about 18 months of continuous learning, practice, and reinforcement to reach a point where he felt he had mastered the principles.

"I can remember the moment when I felt I had passed the Sandler test," he told us. "Our office forwarded a call to me from a particularly aggressive-sounding client who wanted air-conditioning installed in a mansion he had purchased. This was a very successful professional who told me that he had gotten bids from multiple vendors, and he had decided that the job in question should cost him about $8,000. I think he was used to intimidating salespeople. He kept saying, 'That's what it should take. Eight grand.'

"He wanted to know how much we would charge, right then and there on the phone. I told him I couldn't possibly answer his question without knowing anything about the property. At that point he described the home where he wanted air-conditioning installed. I could tell it was a massive job.

"I knew what he wanted me to do, which was to start bargaining with him over the phone around that $8,000 figure. And that's probably what I would have done before I learned the Sandler principles, before I learned about being nurturingly assertive.

"But what I said to him was, 'Well, I can't give you a quote until I see the property in person, but based on what you're telling me, this job is going to be well north of $25,000. If you think you can get it done for $8,000, it doesn't sound like we have anything to talk about. Is there any reason we should continue the conversation?'

"And then I shut up, which is something else I wouldn't have done without the Sandler training. I didn't rescue him. And the next words out of his mouth were, 'When can you come down?'

"He ended up going with us. That's when I knew I'd passed the test. But it took 18 months of reinforcement to get me there. Just knowing the content cognitively wasn't enough. It had to be reinforced in an ongoing way. The time commitment was so important."

From that point forward, Buckwalter was on an upward trajectory. He was soon pulling down an annual income that placed him among the highest-earning HVAC salespeople in North America. **Today, he holds an ownership stake in the company and serves in a senior executive capacity as its operations manager!**

Today, both Buckwalter and his partner Scott Rohrer emphasize that their loyalty to Sandler principles is based not just on sales performance—although that is stellar—but also on the power of holistic implementation of the Sandler principles throughout the enterprise.

"What a lot of people don't realize," Scott told us, "is that this is not just a sales department solution. Sandler is really about life skills, not just sales tactics. How do you tap into the power of the individual and unleash it? How do you support good peer-to-peer discussions? How do you master the art of getting to well-qualified decisions that make sense to both sides? None of that is limited to the world of sales."

Scott gave us an excellent example of the universal applicability of the Sandler principles. He pointed out that capitalizing on a new sales opportunity, collecting on an overdue invoice, and conducting an effective employee evaluation discussion *all* benefit from use of the Sandler Up-Front Contract, by which two parties agree to the goals and ground rules of a discussion before beginning it. "That one technique," Scott observed, "the Up-Front Contract, is deeply relevant to absolutely everything we do: customer service, tech, accounting, sales, interdepartmental communications, all of it. We use it to create win-win opportunities throughout the company, day in and day out."

Scott's son Dustan Rohrer works as an electrician for the company, and he continues to go through the Sandler reinforcement training. That makes three generations of Sandler alumni at Rohrer!

Results

- 300+ percent increase in annual gross revenue compared to 1993
- 100 percent workforce growth since 1993
- Two new businesses acquired since 1993
- Consistently high customer (4.5 out of 5 to 5 out of 5) average rankings on Yelp.com and Businessfinder.Pennlive.com
- Zero turnover among customer service professionals over the past 12 months
- Over 1,700 extended service contracts sold in a recent 3-month period, most by technicians and customer service professionals

Sure Systems: "Everyone in the Organization Needs a Little Sandler."

Company Description

Sure Systems is a local provider of information technology consulting and management services located in Calgary, Alberta. The company specializes in providing IT services to small- and medium-sized organizations.

Accolades

The company was recently a finalist for the Calgary Chamber of Commerce Small Business of the Year, and it is a licensed partner of Microsoft, HP, Lenovo, IBM, CA Technologies, EMC, Citrix, and VMWare.

Key Challenges

In late 2012, CEO and sole salesperson Alex McGillivray found himself stuck at a personal and professional roadblock. He began weekly coaching sessions with Sandler.

"Before I started working with Sandler," McGillivray said, "I was floundering, and so was my company. I was not producing the results I wanted to in terms of revenue. I felt like I was treading water pretty much all the time.

"Our company was already committed to a principal-led selling model, where I was the only salesperson. The irony was that I, as the principal, was uncomfortable with the whole idea of selling. I never even liked thinking of myself as a sales guy. I was an engineer. Selling had always been kind of a dirty word to me. It was all about pressuring other people, and I didn't really want to pressure people. But I felt like that's what I had to do to close deals. I was overwhelmed, overworked, behind my goal, and in a rut."

McGillivray came to Sandler looking for help in the following areas:

- Increase sales performance
- Reduce personal stress
- Shorten sales cycles
- Reduce average working week hours

Business Challenge

As McGillivray recalls: "I was my own worst enemy. I was stressing out myself and everyone else in the company, spending too much of my time chasing proposals that went nowhere, and basically doing whatever prospects told me to do. I was jumping through every hoop they put up, and I was collecting a lot of 'wait and see' responses for my trouble. So that was all pretty stressful.

"Very early on, my Sandler trainer shared some critical principles for dealing with this kind of problem, which is something a lot of salespeople go through. One of the most important of those principles was the Up-Front Contract.

"Establishing an Up-Front Contract means setting up clear agreements ahead of time for what's going to happen in the meeting. I saw that part of the reason I wasn't getting clear yes or no answers was that I wasn't setting any meaningful ground rules in the relationship as it got started. So I started working on that.

"I started having weekly coaching sessions with Sandler in November 2012. Those weekly sessions transformed my whole approach to selling. The part I want to emphasize here is the word 'weekly.' This wasn't just about reading a book or memorizing a few scripts or a few concepts. This was ongoing reinforcement, leading to major behavioral changes. It took ongoing interaction with my Sandler trainer to change my communication patterns.

"It took a weekly commitment for me to reach a point where I was good at creating low-pressure exchanges in which both sides could identify a positive outcome. But it was worth it. And I've kept it up.

"The closest thing I can compare my Sandler training to is my own experience in the world of martial arts. Just understanding a new karate move, just seeing it and knowing what it's called, is not the same as being able to perform it properly during a sparring session. It takes time and practice and repetition and reinforcement to get to that point. With enough practice, you reach a point where you aren't thinking about the move, and you aren't even performing the move—you are the move. You've internalized it. It's part of who you are.

"It's the same with Sandler. It took me about six months of coaching sessions to get to that point with the Sandler 'moves.' It took weekly communication, weekly goals, weekly accountability. My Sandler coach was big on accountability, and I was grateful for that.

"Sandler is all about supporting you as you develop new behavior patterns, new attitudes, and new tactics. I guess the biggest, most obvious positive change for me has been that I now get to a yes or no answer much more quickly. That has made a huge difference in terms of the length of our sales cycle, which is now considerably shorter. Our opportunity size is now larger too. That means the company's income picture is a lot brighter than it was a year ago!

"A completely unexpected benefit has been reduced turnover at our company. The Up-Front Contract and the other Sandler principles have made me a better manager, and they have led to some positive cultural changes at our company. I've shared the principles with everyone on our staff.

"I know there are a lot of people, engineering and accounting and legal people and so on, who are skeptical about both sales and about sales training. I would just say to them that the Sandler System is really about communication. And what I figured out is that everyone in the organization needs a little Sandler."

Results

- Overall gross quarterly margin increased from 16.6 to 49.7 percent.
- Earnings before interest, tax, depreciation, and amortization were 2.0 percent of sales in 2012, and 9.5 percent of sales in the first 11 months of 2013.
- CEO's average workweek went from over 60 hours to less than 40 hours.
- Sales cycle grew shorter.
- Average opportunity grew larger.
- Annual company turnover went down by 67 percent.

TDIndustries: "We Changed the Game. Now We Don't Waste Time on Bad Deals or Chase RFPs the Way Our Competitors Do."

Company Description

TDIndustries is one of America's largest and most respected mechanical construction and facility services companies.

Accolades

Included in "The 100 Best Companies to Work for in America" by bestselling business authors Robert Levering and Milton Moskowitz. Named a National Ernst & Young Entrepreneur of the Year Award for Principle-Centered Leadership winner.

Key Challenges

The need to empower its sales force to proactively seek new business rather than simply managing accounts that found their way to the door.

TDIndustries, a 65-year-old company with an ambitious 10-year growth plan, had a problem. Meeting the plan was going to be next to impossible without a drastic adjustment to its sales model. TD's sales force was taking a reactive approach rather than a proactive one, focusing on managing and selling to existing customers rather than aggressively seeking new ones.

In order to meet its growth plan, the construction side of TD's business needed to double over 10 years, and its service side needed to triple. TD didn't have a process or a program in place to make that happen. One thing it did have was the knowledge that it needed world-class sales training, and fast. That's when Sandler entered the picture.

Sandler Solution

We started off by doing a lot of listening. We heard about TD's pain, talked about its struggles, asked a lot of questions, and then we got to work creating a customized plan for its sales team.

The plan, which honored the fact that every customer is different, took a multifocused approach that included the following:

- Boot camps for both its sales force and its sales leadership, designed to help them understand the Sandler Selling System— why it works and how it works
- Monthly webinars covering specific sales topics
- Quarterly reinforcement training that allowed Sandler principles to become second nature to TD's sales force over time, resulting in lasting changes rather than ineffective quick fixers
- Accountability benchmarks identified by TD sales leaders with guidance from Sandler trainers
- Sales certification program to keep TD's sales team working toward its goals

Results

We gave TD's sales professionals a scientific, methodical approach to selling. We combined it with tools to guide them step-by-step through every new business opportunity. In less than three years, the company's sales conversion rates went from 5 to 50 percent.

The business units that truly embraced the Sandler System had absolutely no problems in hitting their sales goals—indeed, hitting them for the very first time.

From a cultural perspective, TD's experience with Sandler has been significant. "Life is much better than it was before from a financial reward perspective and an empowerment perspective," says one TD executive.

In the words of another, "We changed the game. Now we don't waste time on bad deals or chase requests for proposals (RFPs) the way our competitors do. We create opportunities, and Sandler made all the difference in helping us do that."

B

APPLYING THE SANDLER PRINCIPLES TO THE ENTERPRISE SELLING ENVIRONMENT

Sandler Enterprise Selling Program

Enterprise sales are typically those featuring multiple decision makers and influencers, longer sales cycles, and the coordination of multiple work groups on both the buying side and the selling side. There are six stages to the Sandler Enterprise Selling (SES) program, which incorporates all the principles of the familiar Sandler Submarine. An executive overview of each SES stage follows.

For more information on the SES program, call 410-559-2003 or visit www.sandler.com/enterpriseselling.

Stage One: Territory and Account Planning

In enterprise selling, there is a great deal that must happen before you reach out to a prospect or client about a specific opportunity. The critical first step is planning. The five phases of effective planning in enterprise selling are:

- Market understanding
- Analysis/SWOT assessment
- Client/Prospect profile development
- Development of territory value propositions and action plans
- Account planning

Each of these phases is covered in detail in this first stage of the Sandler Enterprise Selling program. Territory planning is the focus of the first four phases. Account planning, the fifth phase, focuses on individual accounts.

Key areas to focus on in the market understanding phase are the account base, economy, service and deployment structure, market trends/patterns, and competition.

Once the relevant information is collected, it must be analyzed and assessed. The SWOT Tool provides a structured framework to evaluate your findings in light of both internal and external factors.

In the profile development phase, you will use the **KARE (Keep, Attain, Recapture, Expand) Profiling Tool** to develop pro forma territory value propositions to add significant substance to territory planning and to provide the basis for customer-focused decision making that will eventually move the process forward.

With the clarity gained up to this point about the market and prospects, alignment to your product/service is the next key step. Even before you begin to identify specific accounts and opportunities, you will create territory value propositions that serve as a bridge from your offerings to the prospect base.

As the complexity and sophistication of clients continue to increase, the need for an integrated framework to drive customer retention and expansion is critical. In the account planning fifth phase, the **Growth Account Booster Tool** incorporates the four key elements of account planning—account profiling, decision network analysis, targeted opportunity focus, and action strategy. The team selling structure of this highly effective account management tool brings to bear all of the key resources in a selling organization that maximize the likelihood of success and client growth.

Stage Two: Opportunity Identification

Opportunity Identification is the second stage of the Sandler Enterprise Selling program. This stage gives you the tools you need to prospect effectively, engage with prospects, communicate with them to deliver valued insights in a compelling way, and set mutual expectations.

Businesses and salespeople alike are constantly in need of new clients. This is true even for the salesperson who works only a few accounts, or even a single account. For this salesperson, the "new client" initially takes the form of a new prospect, that is, a new opportunity that can move the relationship forward. Within any existing account are multiple new prospects. Each client is actually a new marketplace unto itself!

Attitude, Behavior, and Technique are three triangles connected to the famous Sandler Success triangle. You need all three to achieve success. For example, having a positive attitude accomplishes little or nothing if that attitude isn't channeled into an effectively executed plan. By the same token, even the best behavior plans are doomed to fail if they are not backed by a supportive attitude and implemented with the requisite skills. And technique alone won't accomplish much unless it's applied to an appropriate framework of behavior with a positive expectation of success.

The **LinkedIn Levers Tool** will help you leverage the substantial power of this online business networking site in support of your prospecting goals.

When it comes to face-to-face communication, words can mislead and tonality can conceal intent, but the body never lies! "DISC" is a well-known behavioral model used to categorize the way people interact with one another. The **Relationship Builder Tool** will help you create strong connections with key enterprise contacts.

A critical element for maintaining efficiency in the business development process is to keep the process moving forward. Opportunities that become stalled can drain resources, including time, the most precious resource of all. Therefore, each sales interaction, whether face-to-face or via the phone, needs to be focused on a mutually agreed-to objective, with both you and your prospect working toward a mutually beneficial outcome that drives the process forward.

The Up-Front Contract is an essential communication tool that helps establish mutual responsibilities and expectations, and it keeps the sales process moving forward. The **Three Opportunity Planner Tool** provides a clear focus on the three highest-probability opportunities that are likely to close within the next 60 days.

Stage Three: Qualification

In stage three, you will learn how to qualify deals in a way that clarifies, for both sides, whether it really makes sense to proceed.

An essential component of corporate planning is ongoing competitive analysis, which helps you fortify both your offensive and defensive strategies. The **Positioning Tool** will help you to develop a clearer understanding of your competition and the best ways to position your offer against theirs. Much of the essential information you need to know about your competition is readily available if you invest a little time and open yourself up to the possibility of searching for information shrewdly.

Team selling is fundamental to the Sandler Enterprise Selling program because enterprise organizations employ a team buying process. Here in stage three, you will create your own selling team based on what you know about the buying team.

The **Pre-Call Planner Tool** and the **Call Debrief Tool** give you a process for conducting and taking action on the discussions that will help you to qualify prospects.

Pain is the gap between what the prospect has—the existing condition—and what the prospect wants or needs—typically, a more desirable condition. The prospect's perception of the problem usually does not reflect the actual problem—its underlying causes and contributing factors. The **Opportunity Tool** will help you to identify critical budget and financial concerns, obstacles to organizational performance, and the personal career objectives of the prospect/customer.

You can use the questioning strategies you find in stage three to uncover the reasons for the problem—the real pain—and determine whether you can fix it. Uncovering the impact of the problem will give you an indication of both the severity of the problem and the prospect's commitment to fix it.

Uncovering the amount of funding that prospects are both willing and able to invest is critical in the qualifying stage. If they can't or won't commit the size investment required for you to deliver the appropriate solution to their pains, then they should be disqualified.

Your ability to uncover good information is directly related to your comfort level in regard to discussing money matters. If you're uncomfortable, perhaps because of early childhood programming, then having a prepared questioning strategy to fall back on can ease your discomfort. Three strategies can make it easier to discuss money: direct questions, third-party stories, and bracketing questions.

Stage Four: Solution Development

After all the work you put in thus far, you have earned the right to move ahead with the preparation and crafting of a solution for the prospect that uniquely qualifies your product/service to win the business. You have done your initial research into all of the relevant variables involving the prospect and the opportunity, and you have received the prospect's concurrence to proceed, as a partner, in the process. You have also consistently reviewed the pursuit in terms of the relevant go/no-go factors from your side. Having done all that, you are ready for this important stage.

In stage four, you will learn to use the **Pursuit Navigator Tool** to support sound go/no-go decisions that are rooted in quantifiable metrics and business logic. You will also learn to work with the prospect to craft a viable solution, and you will make a seamless transition into the Proposing and Advancement stage.

Stage Five: Proposing and Advancement

In stage four, Solution Development, you laid the groundwork for proposal development. Moving forward from Solution Development's Build and Form step, you now begin actively developing the proposal, driving the solution developed for the enterprise prospect organization to a final form, typically via a formal proposal.

In this fifth stage, you will identify and execute the team activities involved in finalizing the proposal document. A team leader must be chosen for the presentation team. Often, this will be the sales lead—the person with the strongest relationship to the account. It's also critical that the leader is a person with extensive group presentation experience as he or she must act as an observer and coach, helping the presenters anticipate issues and problems that might arise.

During this stage, the client's needs and pains must always be at the forefront of your thinking. Your organization's past experiences and precedents should not lead the conversation. Focus the content on the unique client with whom you are dealing, avoiding the reuse of archived assets that may not be targeted to the relevant needs and pains you have uncovered. Practice proposal delivery relentlessly.

After a loss, schedule a debriefing and conduct a postmortem.

After a win, move on to contract finalization. Do not broadcast your victory. Be prepared for surprises, and stand your ground.

Stage Six: Service Delivery

After all the time, money, and effort you invested to pursue this opportunity, it is time to focus keenly on service excellence and delivering effectively now that the business is won. And by the way, if you lost the business in interactions with this client in the past, but won this time around, now is the time to prove the saying "Failure is a bruise, not a tattoo."

If you communicate effectively during this all-important phase, you can not only make this engagement successful, but you can also expand the business relationship over time. Too many selling organizations underemphasize the importance of a coordinated, team-driven, information-rich approach to service delivery. This may well be the most important stage of all, because it is the one most likely to lead to additional business from this company or one allied to it.

Superior service, based on the customer's criteria, is the best client retention program there is. In this stage, you will learn to use the **Customer-Centric Satisfaction Tool,** the **Growth Account Booster Tool,** and the **Team Storm Tool** in support of the goal of superior service.

In addition, you will learn to leverage the relationships you've established to uncover even more opportunities. The **Client² Tool** will help you with this. There is no better time to win additional business than after you've won business.

INDEX